PLUTO
Dia. 1,860 mi.
3,000 km.
Rot. 6.39 days
Dist. from Sun 3,706,780,000 mi.
5,965,200,000 km.

Rev. 247 yrs.
Moons †

URANUS
Dia. 32,600 mi.
52,400 km.
Rot. 16 hrs.
Dist. from Sun 1,783,170,000 mi.
2,869,600,000 km.

Rev. 84.01 yrs.
Moons 5
Rings 9
Dia. 59,700 mi.
96,000 km.

mi.
km.

SATURN
Dia. 75,100 mi.
121,000 km.
Rot. 10.67 hrs.
Dist. from Sun 886,740,000 mi.
1,427,000,000 km.

Rev. 29.46 yrs.
Moons 21, possibly 23
Ring System
More than 1,000 ringlike
features in 6 distinct bands
Dia. 177,100 mi.
285,000 km.

RS
4,212 mi.
6,778 km.
24.62 hrs.
from Sun 141,680,000 mi.
228,000,000 km.

1.88 yrs.
ns 2

Andromeda Galaxy

Rand McNally
Children's
World
Atlas

Rand McNally & Company
Chicago • New York • San Francisco

Contents

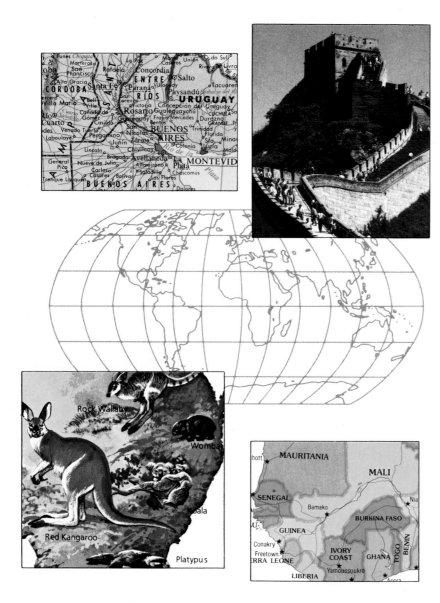

Rand McNally Children's World Atlas
Copyright © 1989 by Rand McNally &
Company

Printed in Italy.
Library of Congress Catalog Card Number:
88-061950
ISBN: 528-83348-0

World maps, pages 14-19, from *Rand
McNally Classroom Atlas*, copyright © 1988.
Other maps, photos, illustrations from
Rand McNally Student's World Atlas,
copyrights © 1988, 1982; and *Rand McNally
Children's Atlas of the World*, copyrights
© 1985, 1979.

Using the Atlas

An atlas is a guide to the world that can be used in many ways. But to discover the world with your atlas, you must be able to do five things:

- Measure distances using a map scale.
- Use directions and latitude and longitude.
- Find places on the maps using map keys.
- Use different kinds of maps.
- Use map symbols and legends.

The following sections can help you learn how to do these things.

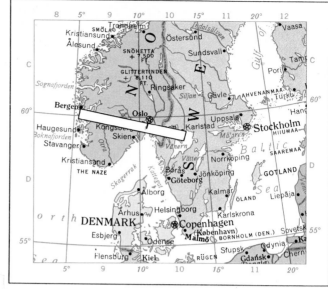

Figure 1

Measuring Distances

To understand a map, you must know its *scale,* or how large an area of the earth it shows. There are different types of map scales, but the *bar scale* is the easiest to use for finding distance.

For example, to find the distance between Bergen and Oslo in Norway, first you will find out how far Bergen is from Oslo on the map. Then, by using a bar scale, you will learn what this means in actual distance on the earth.

1. Find Bergen and Oslo on the map in Figure 1.
2. Lay a slip of paper on the map so its edge touches the two cities. Move the paper so one corner touches Bergen.
3. Mark the paper where it touches Oslo. The distance from the corner of the paper to the mark shows how far Oslo is from Bergen on the map.
4. The numbers in the map scale in Figure 2 show *statute miles,* or miles on the earth. Line up the edge of the paper along the map scale, putting the corner at 0.
5. Find the mark on the paper. The

mark shows that Bergen is about two hundred miles away from Oslo.

Using Directions and Latitude and Longitude

Most of the maps in this atlas are drawn so north is at the top of the page, south is at the bottom, west is at the left, and east is at the right.

Many of the maps also have lines drawn across them — lines of *latitude* and *longitude.* These are lines drawn on a map or globe to make it easier to tell directions and to find places.

As shown in Figure 3, lines of latitude run east and west. The equator is a line of latitude, and it runs around the middle of the earth. Other lines of latitude are used to measure how far north or south of the equator a place is. Lines of latitude are numbered in *degrees,* which measure the distance. The equator is at zero degrees (0°) latitude. The numbers go up in each direction (north and south) the farther you get from the equator. The map in Figure 1 shows that Bergen is north of sixty degrees (60°) latitude and Stockholm is

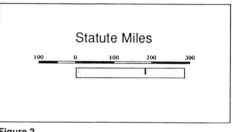

Statute Miles

| 100 | 0 | 100 | 200 | 300 |

Figure 2

Figure 3

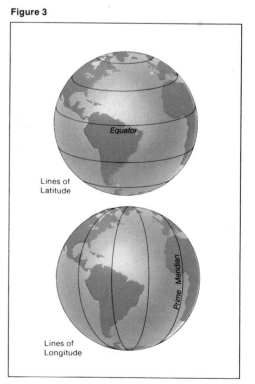

Equator

Lines of Latitude

Prime Meridian

Lines of Longitude

south of it. So Bergen is farther north than Stockholm.

Lines of longitude run north and south between the two poles, as you can see from Figure 3. Like latitude, longitude is measured in degrees. The *prime meridian* is at zero degrees (0°) longitude. Lines of longitude measure how far east or west a place is from the prime meridian. The numbers go up as you go in each direction (east and west). In Figure 1, Bergen is about five degrees (5°) east of the prime meridian, and Stockholm is about twenty degrees (20°). So Stockholm is farther east than Bergen.

Using Map Keys

One of the most important things an atlas can do is tell you the location of a place. To help you find a place quickly and easily on a map, most atlases have an index that includes the names of places and a guide that is made up of a letter and a number, or a *map key*.

Say you want to find Santiago, a city in Chile, which is in South America. Here's how you would use the map key.

1. Look up the city's name, Santiago, in the back of the atlas. You see an entry like the one in Figure 4. The number 88 is the page on which the map is found. The map key C2 is the letter-number guide to finding Santiago on the map on page 88.

Figure 4

2. Look at Figure 5. It is a piece of the map of southern South America that is on page 88.
3. Find the letters A through C along the left-hand side of the map. Then find the numbers 2 through 4 along the top edge of the map. These numbers and letters are centered between the lines of latitude and longitude on the map.
4. To find Santiago, use the map key C2. Place your left index finger on C and your right index finger on 2. Move your left finger across the map and your right finger down the map, staying within the latitude and longitude lines on either side. Your fingers will meet in the box in which Santiago is located.

You can use this method to find any place listed in the index of this atlas. If you see a small, or *lowercase*, letter in a map key, it refers to the small inset map on the page rather than to the main map on the page. Two map keys are shown for areas that begin on one map and continue on another map.

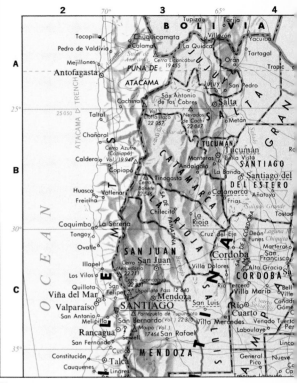

Figure 5

Distance between meridians shrinks near the North and South poles. At the equator, a giraffe would have to run seventy miles (112.65 kilometers) to cover one degree of longitude. Near the South Pole, a penguin could merely wiggle a toe over the ice and cross a meridian.

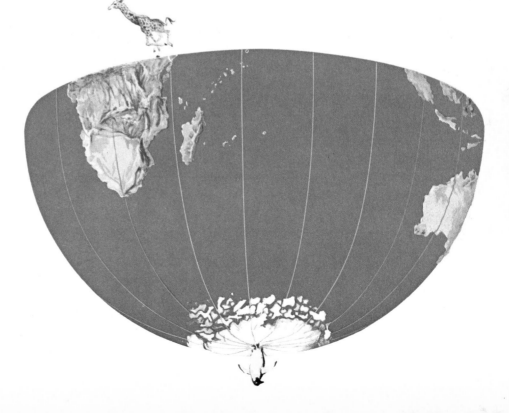

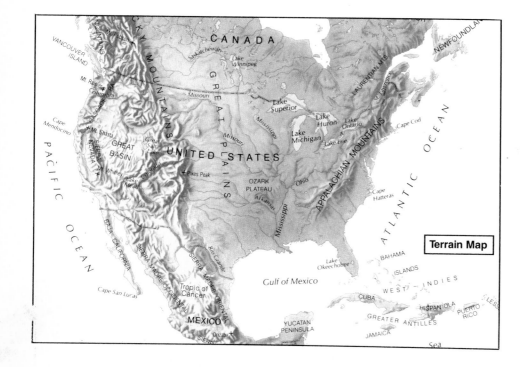

Terrain Map

Using Different Kinds of Maps

There are lots of types of maps, and each type has a different purpose. In this atlas, you will find terrain maps, thematic maps, political maps, and physical-political maps.

The *terrain maps* go along with the terrain sections for each continent. These are also called physical maps because they show only the physical features of the land, such as mountains, rivers, and lakes. On the terrain map of North America, the colors and shading mean that the West has high mountains, the central part is a flat grassland, north of the Great Lakes is forested, and much of central Mexico is desert.

The *thematic maps* go with the sections on animals and life on the land. The thematic maps show pictures that tell you about different regions on the map. On the the-

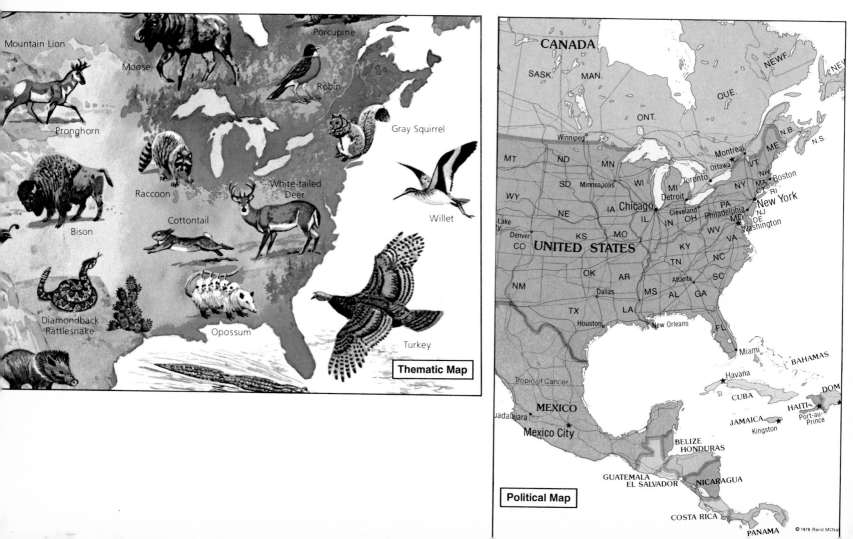

Thematic Map

Political Map

© 1979 Rand McNally

matic map of the animals of North America, you can see that raccoons live around the Great Lakes. The other type of thematic map in this atlas tells what people do in different parts of a continent.

The *political maps* go with the sections about countries and cities. These maps show you the boundaries of each country on the continent as well as the major cities. On the political map of North America, the thickest gray lines are country boundaries. The thinner gray lines are state or province borders. The thinnest gray lines are railroad tracks. The red lines are major roads.

The *physical-political maps* are all by themselves on the pages. These maps tell you the most about each continent. On them you can find physical features, such as rivers and mountains, and you can find human-made features, such as political boundaries of countries

and cities. You can read these maps with the help of a *legend*, which is discussed in the next section.

Using Map Symbols and Legends

A *symbol* is something that stands for something else. In a way, a whole map is a symbol, because it represents the world, or part of it.

A map *legend* explains the symbols used on a map. The legend shown to the right tells about the symbols that are used on the physical-political maps in this atlas. It divides the earth's features into three major classes: cultural, land, and water features. Cultural features are human-made and include cities, roads, railroads, and boundaries. Land features include mountain peaks, mountain passes, and *spot heights*, which tell the elevation of certain places on a mountain. Water features include rivers, lakes, swamps, and other kinds of bodies of water.

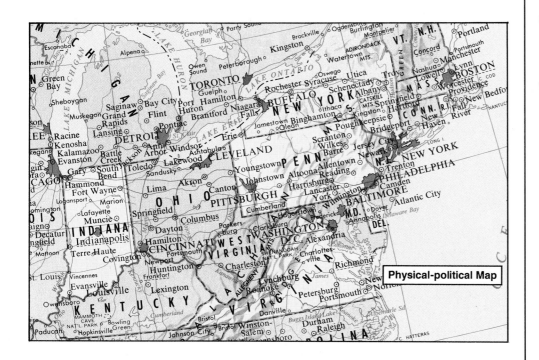

Physical-political Map

PHYSICAL-POLITICAL MAP LEGEND

CULTURAL FEATURES

Political Boundaries

International

Intercolonial

Secondary: State, Provincial, etc.

Cities, Towns and Villages
(Except for scales of 1:20,000,000 or smaller)

PARIS — 1,000,000 and over

Ufa — 500,000 to 1,000,000

Győr — 50,000 to 500,000

Agadir — 25,000 to 50,000

Moreno — 0 to 25,000

TŌKYŌ — National Capitals

Boise — Secondary Capitals

Transportation

Railroads

Railroad Ferries

Caravan Routes

Other Cultural Features

Dams

Pipelines

▲ Pyramids

∴ Ruins

LAND FEATURES

△ Peaks, Spot Heights

= Passes

WATER FEATURES

Lakes and Reservoirs

Fresh Water

Fresh Water: Intermittent

Salt Water

Salt Water: Intermittent

Other Water Features

Swamps

Glaciers

Rivers

Canals

Aqueduct — Aqueducts

Ship Channels

Falls

Rapids

Springs

△ Water Depths

Sand Bars

Reefs

World • Terrain

Types of Terrain

Ice and Snow		Tundra and Alpine		High Barren Area
Grassland		Desert		Dry Scrub
Broadleaf Trees		Needleleaf Trees		Tropical Rainforest

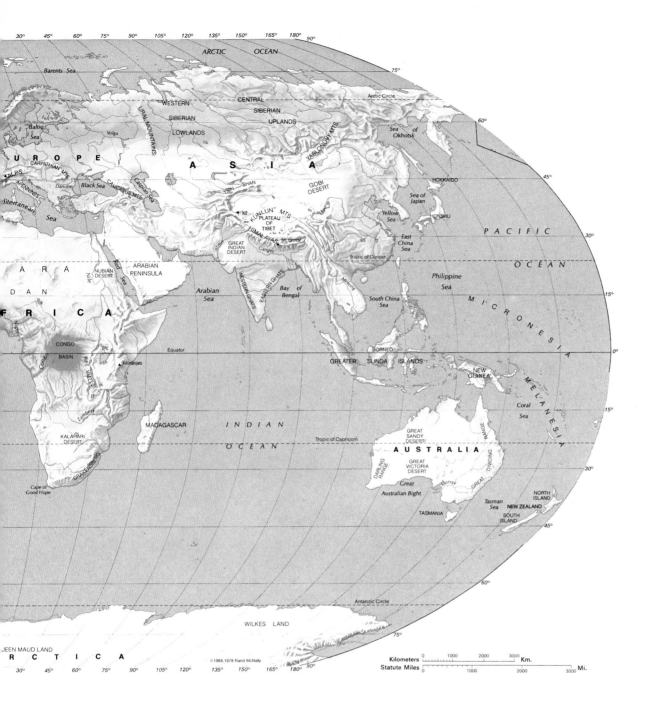

This map shows the terrain of the earth. The colors and shading of the different areas on the map tell you what kind of terrain is found in that area of the world. The legend can help you.

You can easily see where the earth's mountains are. High mountains arose millions of years ago, created by great collisions between the earth's *plates.* These plates are like rafts floating on the earth. Mountains are formed when these gigantic plates collide.

Clearly visible on this map are deserts. Deserts are dry lands with low rainfall and sparse plant and animal life. Not all deserts are hot, sandy, and sunny. Deserts can also be cold, rocky, or snow and ice covered.

The land along the seas of the world is the coast. You can see the many, many coastlines of the world. Because of the effects of water, coastlines are always changing.

You can also see the world's many islands. An island is a body of land that is smaller than a continent and completely surrounded by water.

World · Climate

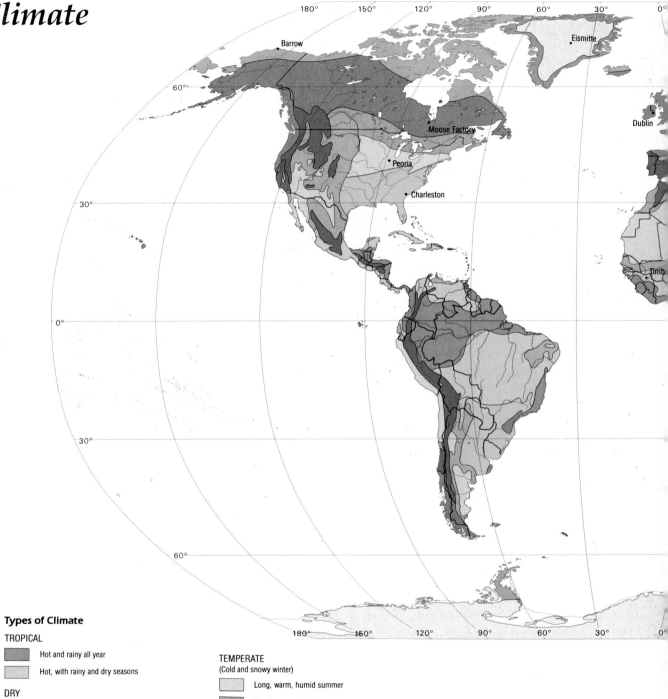

Types of Climate

TROPICAL

- Hot and rainy all year
- Hot, with rainy and dry seasons

DRY

- Desert, with some rain
- Desert

TEMPERATE
(Mild and rainy winter)

- Hot and dry summer
- Warm and humid summer
- Mild and rainy summer

TEMPERATE
(Cold and snowy winter)

- Long, warm, humid summer
- Short, warm, humid summer
- Very short, cool, humid summer

POLAR

- Tundra (very cold and dry)
- Ice cap

HIGHLAND

- Varies with height and latitude

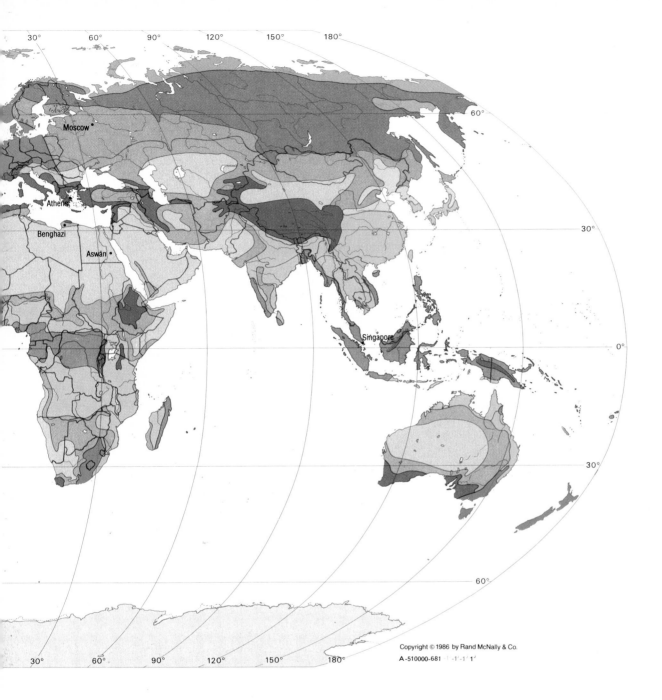

This map shows the climates of the earth. The colors of the different areas on the map tell you what kind of climate is found in that area of the world. The legend can help you.

Climate and weather are not the same thing. *Weather* describes the temperature and *precipitation* — rain, snow, or other moisture — of an area during a short time period. *Climate*, on the other hand, describes the same things but for a much longer period of time. It takes many years to determine a region's climate.

The climate we live in directly affects our lifestyles. From the types of clothing we wear to the kind of food we eat, from the way we travel from one place to another to the kinds of homes we live in — all are dictated by climate.

Climates around the world vary for different reasons. In general, climates are hotter closer to the equator and colder as you go either north or south. Additionally, climates tend to be affected by large bodies of water and by the surface of the land.

World · *Life on the Land*

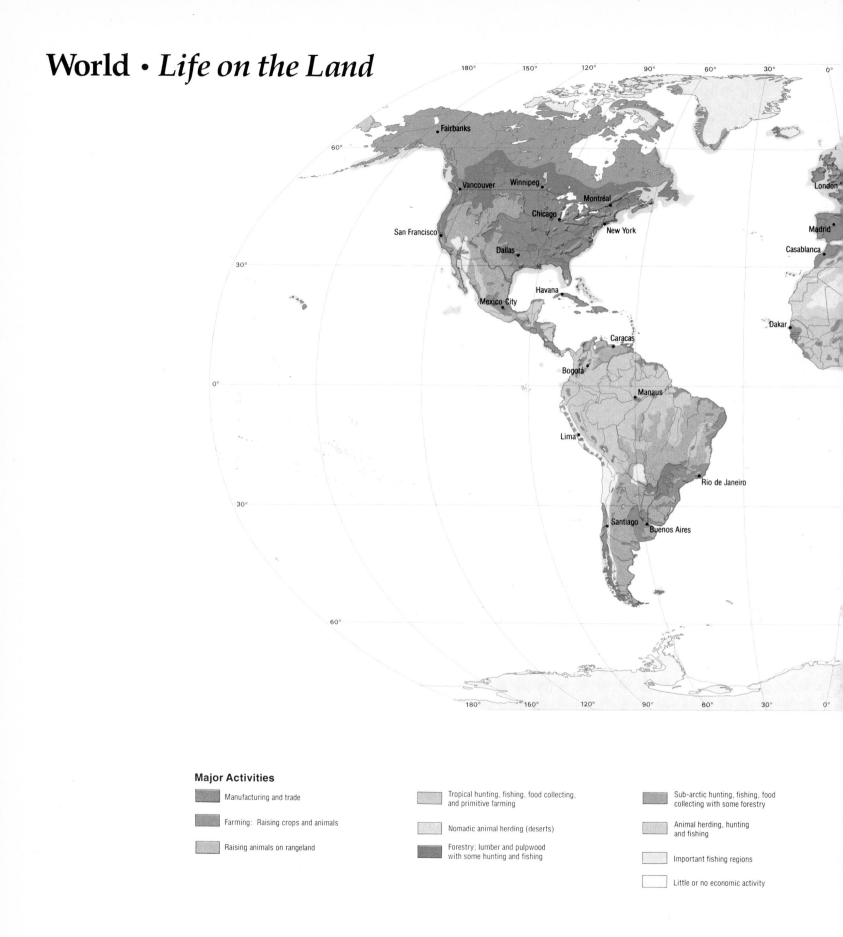

Major Activities

- Manufacturing and trade
- Farming: Raising crops and animals
- Raising animals on rangeland
- Tropical hunting, fishing, food collecting, and primitive farming
- Nomadic animal herding (deserts)
- Forestry; lumber and pulpwood with some hunting and fishing
- Sub-arctic hunting, fishing, food collecting with some forestry
- Animal herding, hunting and fishing
- Important fishing regions
- Little or no economic activity

This map shows the major economic activities of the world. The colors of the different areas on the map tell you what most of the people do for a living in that area of the world. The legend can help you.

The character of the land has much to do with its use. In general, the farmed areas shown on the map are among the most fertile on earth.

You can see that very few regions of the world are used for manufacturing and trade. These areas are sometimes called *developed*, and they become developed for a variety of reasons. In the United States, many developed areas are near natural resources and transportation routes.

You can often tell what the people in an area of the world do by what the land is like. For example, there is usually a lot of fishing along coastlines. But sometimes you cannot predict what people do by the land on which they live. For example, people may live on good farmland, but they may not be able to farm it efficiently. Sometimes there are political reasons for this.

World · *Population*

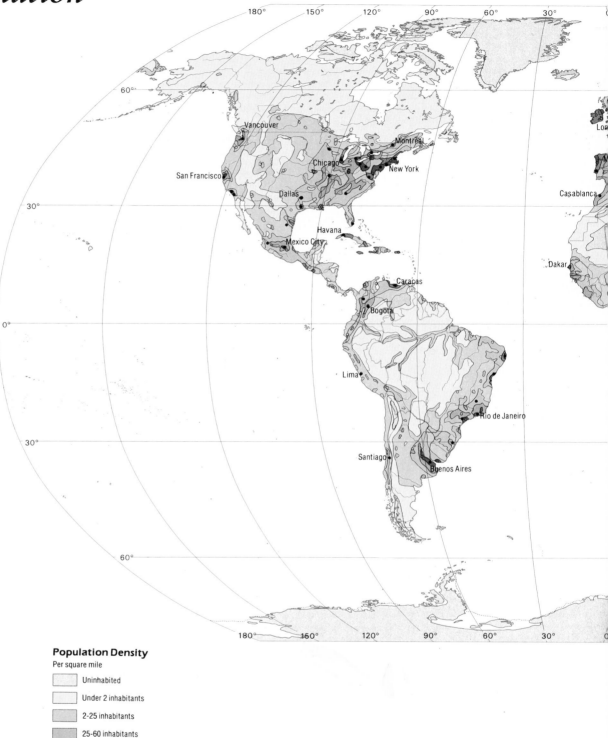

Population Density

Per square mile

	Uninhabited
	Under 2 inhabitants
	2-25 inhabitants
	25-60 inhabitants
	60-125 inhabitants
	125-250 inhabitants
	Over 250 inhabitants
•	Metropolitan areas over 2,000,000 population
○	Metropolitan areas 1,000,000 to 2,000,000 population

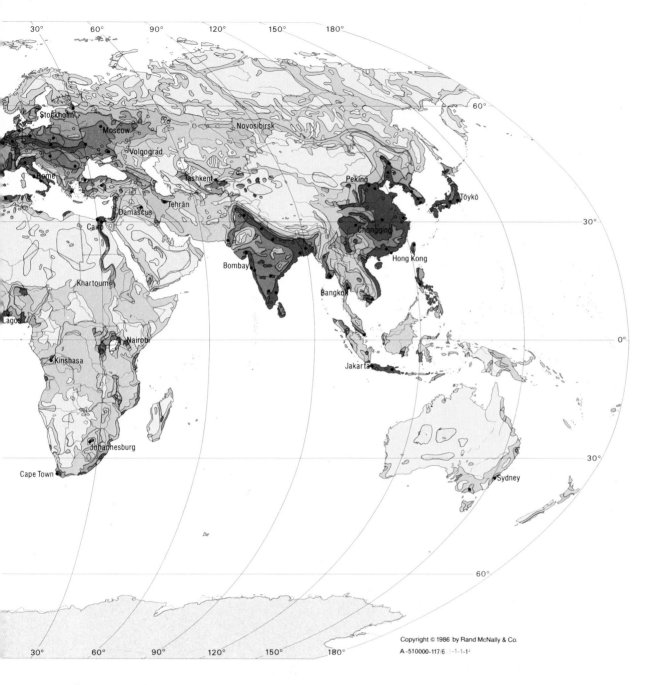

This map shows where people live. The colors of the different areas on the map tell you how many people are found in that area of the world. The legend can help you. *Population density* measures the number of people living in a square mile (about one and a half kilometers).

Densities vary for many reasons, climate and terrain among them. For example, the coldest regions on earth — the areas nearest the North and South poles — are *uninhabited*, meaning that no one lives there. The harsh climate makes set-tlement nearly impossible.

On the other hand, lands with favorable climates and terrains tend to be densely populated, especially if they are good for farming. This is especially true of the crowded parts of India and China.

In other places, such as Europe and the United States, the most densely populated areas tend to be in and around big cities. Often, cities — or *urban* areas — grew up near farmland, resources, and trade routes, especially waterways.

World · Countries

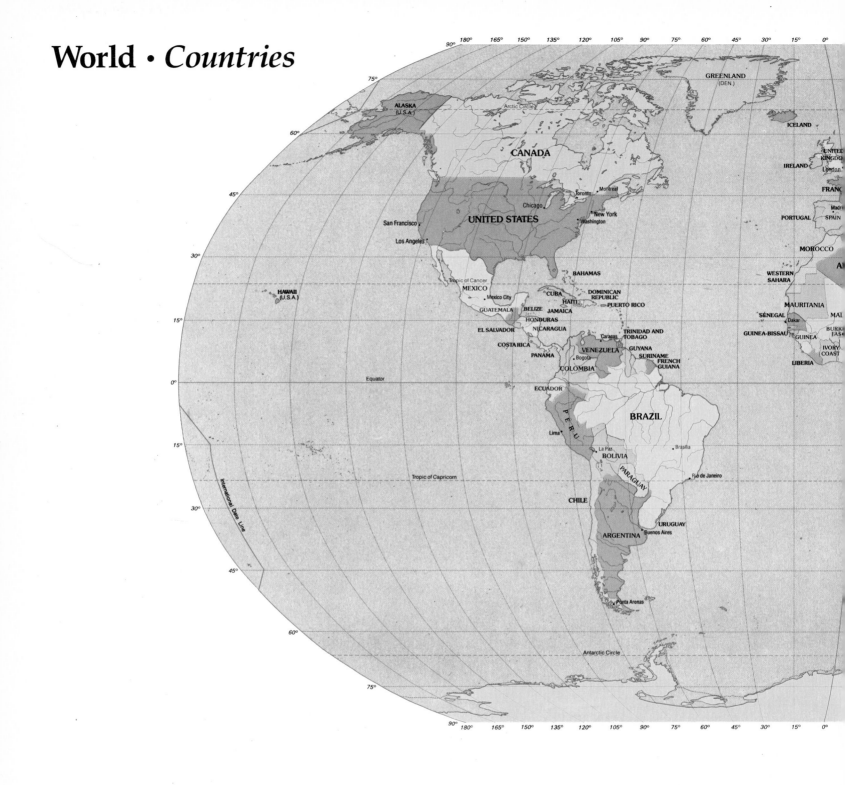

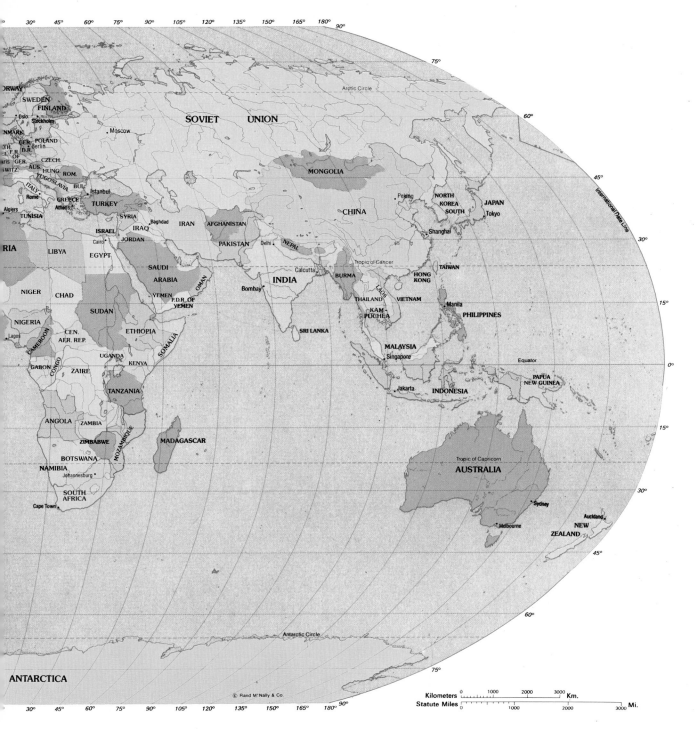

This map shows the countries of the earth. The colors and the lines on the map tell you where the borders of the countries are. The different colors do not tell you anything specific about an area on this map, as they have on other maps.

Often, when people study the world, they organize all the countries into *continents*. Continents are the great divisions of the earth. Nearly all of the continents are big pieces of land that are almost completely surrounded by water.

This atlas divides the world into the seven continents: Europe, Asia, Africa, Australia, North America, South America, and Antarctica. The islands of the South Pacific are grouped with Australia, but they are not part of Australia.

You will see that for each continent — except for Antarctica — there is a section on its *terrain*, or land; a discussion of its wild animals; a section about what the people who live there do for a living; and an overview of its countries and cities.

Europe · *Terrain*

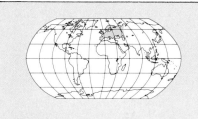

Europe Facts
Sixth largest continent
Second in population: 683,900,000
48 metropolitan areas over 1 million
    population
Highest mountain: Elbrus, 18,510 feet
    (5,642 meters)
Most densely populated continent:
    180 people per square mile
    (69 people per square kilometer)

Many parts of Europe are covered with high mountains. The Alps make up a mountain range that is found in Switzerland, France, Austria, Germany, Italy, and Yugoslavia. Three other mountain ranges spread out from the Alps into other countries. The Appenines reach south into Italy. The Dinaric Alps make a crooked trail through Yugoslavia and Albania and on into Greece. The Carpa-thians tower over much of Czechoslovakia and Romania.

Across the English Channel from mainland Europe are the islands that form the United Kingdom. England lies on the biggest island, and mountains called the Pennines run through that country. To the north is Scotland, with its famous Scottish Highlands.

Northern mainland Europe has many mountains. The land-

scape was once covered by large bodies of solid ice called *glaciers.* These glaciers moved very slowly over the land and carved deep grooves in between the mountains. The grooves flooded with water from the sea and have become long waterways called *fjords.*

To the east of mainland Europe are the Soviet Union's Urals. These mountains are very old. Over many years, wind, rain, and snow have eroded the Urals, so they are not as high as many other mountains.

To the southwest of the Alps, the Pyrenees separate France and Spain. Spain and Portugal lie on a *peninsula,* a body of land that is almost surrounded by water.

Many famous rivers flow from Europe's mountains. The Rhine flows north out of Switzerland, past France, and through Germany and the Netherlands. The Danube is a long river that begins in Germany and flows eastward through seven countries and three capital cities.

The north-central part of Europe is a fertile area known as the Great European Plain. There are farms on this flat land that grow food for Europe and other countries.

Many islands lie to the south of mainland Europe, in the Mediterranean Sea. The warm, sunny beaches of the Mediterranean are popular with tourists.

The Scottish Highlands are rough and rugged, so many Scots live on coastal plains such as this one. Here the land is more easily farmed.

The fjords of Norway and Sweden attract many visitors. Some fjords are more than one hundred miles (160 kilometers) long, and some are nearly four thousand feet (1,200 meters) deep.

Mykonos, at left, and the other Greek islands in the Aegean Sea are part of the Pindus Mountains. Millions of years ago, the sea rose until only the tops of the mountains remained above water.

Caspian Sea

Europe · *Animals*

Skua

Herring

Barnacle Goose

Reindeer

Grey Seal

Wolverine

Lemming

Hare

Basking Shark

Red Deer

Otter

Black Grouse

Pheasant

Badger

Atlantic Salmon

Hedgehog

Rabbit

Fox

Red-legged Partridge

Chamois

Moorhen

Marmot

Stork

Squirrel

Great Bustard

Barbary Ape

Sole

Ferruginous Duck

Hoopoe

Spanish Mackerel

Raven

Whimbrel

Brown Bear

Pine Marten

Wild Boar

Wolf

Griffon Vulture

Roe Deer

Lesser Spotted Eagle

Tur

Octopus

Conger Eel

Most of the forests that once covered much of Europe were cut down long ago to make room for farms, cities, and towns. Many animals lived in those forests, and when the forests disappeared, so did the animals. Many animals were hunted by people until they became extinct. Some of the bigger animals survive today, however, in places that are too remote for people or in places where the animals are legally protected.

Shaggy wild boars with curved tusks can be found in the forests of central Europe. Packs of wolves still live in some places, and in the northern Soviet Union, the huge brown bear still lumbers about. In northern Sweden, Norway, Finland, and in the western Soviet Union, people have tamed reindeer and herd them like cattle.

Many smaller types of animals live in Europe. Foxes, badgers, moles, rabbits, and squirrels are found in many places. The hedgehog is common in northern Europe. It has short, sharp spikes all over its back, like the quills of a porcupine only much thicker.

Small, striped wildcats live in parts of Yugoslavia and Bulgaria. A larger wildcat, the Spanish lynx, lives in Spain.

Sparrows, thrushes, finches, nightingales, and ravens are found throughout central Europe. So are large birds of prey such as falcons and eagles. During the summer, the big white stork is a common sight in cities of the Netherlands, Belgium, and Germany, where it nests on the chimneys of houses.

In a protected forest of Poland, many *wisents* — the bison of prehistoric Europe — live as they have for thousands of years. Full grown, wisents are six feet (almost two meters) tall.

Europe · *Life on the Land*

Fishing

Hydrothermal Plant

Reindeer Herding

Coal Mining

Lumbering

Fishing

Agricultural Area

Canneries

Papermaking

Dairyland

Fishing

Offshore Oil Drilling

Cheese Making

Dairyland

Troika
(3-horse Sleigh)

Agricultural Area

Agricultural Area

Heavy Industry

Houses of Parliament

Heavy Industry (Steel)

Farming

Dairyland

Eiffel Tower

Bulb Farming

Grimm's Fairy Tale
Country

Oil Fields

Vineyards

Citrus Groves

Export by Sea

Matterhorn

Wheatlands

Light
Industry

Cork Harvesting

Sheep Raised

Water Sports

Roman Ruins

Olive Orchards

Bullfighting

Opera

Olive Orchards

Vineyards

Ancient Greek Ruins

Fishing

Vineyards

Look at the map of Europe. You can see that the whole continent sticks out into the sea. Water is everywhere. In fact, no part of western Europe is more than three hundred miles from the sea. It is no wonder that many Europeans depend on fishing or sailing to make their living.

Between the many mountains of Europe lie most of Europe's farms. More than half of the land of Europe is used for farming, and about one-sixth of the people are farmers. Vineyards cover many of the hilly areas of France, Germany, Spain, and Italy. Most of the world's olives are grown in Spain, Italy, and Greece. On the flatter lands of Europe, farmers grow barley, oats, potatoes, rye, sugar beets, and wheat.

The raising of livestock is also important. Many farmers raise cattle, hogs, sheep, and poultry for meat. Dairy farming is especially important in Denmark, Great Britain, and the Netherlands.

Modern industry, especially mining and manufacturing, began in Europe. Today, many world industrial leaders are European nations, including the eastern Soviet Union, West Germany, France, Great Britain, Italy, and Poland.

Europe is smaller than any other continent except for Australia. But, it has more people than any other continent except for Asia. As a result, Europe is very densely populated. Even though the people live close together, the many different countries of Europe have their own cultures.

Europe • *Countries and Cities*

Europe has seen many wars, most of them fought over pieces of land. Thus, the boundaries of countries have shifted many times over the centuries. Most recently, World Wars I and II caused boundary changes in several existing countries, and several new nations were formed as well.

Usually, the borders of countries form around natural barriers, such as rivers, seas, or mountain ranges. The reason for this is these are places where people can easily defend themselves from attack. When people first settle an area, they look for such natural barriers. Many countries still are edged by such natural borders, including many European countries.

Today, many western European countries elect their lead-

ers. In some countries, the descendants of the kings and queens that ruled most European countries in earlier times are still treated as royalty, but they do not rule the country.

Several countries in eastern Europe have communist governments. In these countries, the government owns the businesses, and there tend to be more controls over people's

Rome once ruled most of Europe and surrounding areas. These are the remains of the Roman Forum, still standing after more than two thousand years. The Forum was the center of Roman government as well as a marketplace and meeting place.

RUSSIA

Gor'kiy

UNION
PORTION)

Kuybyshev

Volgograd

© 1979 Rand McNally & Co.

lives. These countries maintain close ties with the Soviet Union.

Something travelers going through Europe notice is its many languages. Latin-speaking Romans once conquered much of Europe; today the French, Italians, Spanish, Portuguese, and Romanians speak different languages that are based on ancient Latin. The people of Germany, the Netherlands, England, Denmark, Sweden, and Norway speak different languages that are rooted in old German. To the east, the peoples of Poland,

Czechoslovakia, Yugoslavia, Bulgaria, and the Soviet Union all speak languages based on Slavic dialects.

Europe has many big cities that are rich in history and culture. Athens, Greece, is a very old city with many ancient buildings. So is Rome, Italy. In ancient times, Romans founded some European cities that remain important today, including London, England, and Paris, France. The capital cities of most other European countries tend to be fairly large and modern.

———— Roads
········· Railroads

Scale 1:16,850,000 ; one inch to 265 miles. Conic Projection

Elevations and depressions are given in feet

Scale 1:21,500,000; one inch to 340 miles.
Lambert's Azimuthal, Equal Area Projection
Elevations and depressions are given in feet

33

A   B   17   18   19   C

40,000 SQ. MI.
AREA

0   150   300
Miles

A   9   10   11   12   13   14   15   16   B   17   18   19   C

C

SEVERNAYA ZEMLYA
(NORTHERN LAND)

DE-LONGA

NOVOSIBIRSKIYE O-VA
(NEW SIBERIAN ISLANDS)

CHUKOTSKIY
P-OV

VRANGELYA
(WRANGEL)

ARCTIC   OCEAN

LAPTEV
SEA

EAST   SIBERIAN   SEA

CHUKOTSKOYE NAGOR'YE

KORYAKSKIY KHREBET

D

TAYMYR
P-OV
GORY   BYRRANGA

KOTEL'NYY

M. CHELYUSKIN

Nordvik

M. SVYATOY
NOS

M. SHELAGSKIY

Ambarchik

Nizhne-Kolymsk

Markovo

Penzhino

KAMCHATKA

Ust'-Kamchatsk

Noril'sk

GORY
PUTORANA

Igarka

Khatanga

Ust'-Olenek

Tiksi

Bulun

Kazach'ye

Zashiversk

Zyryanka

Srednekolymsk

KHREBET GYDAN (KOLYMSKIY)

Magadan

Verkhne-Kamchatsk

Petropavlovsk-
Kamchatskiy

Turukhansk

Nizhnyaya Tunguska

Tura

Olenek

Zhigansk

Verkhoyansk

Gora Gha
10,171

Oymyakon

Okhotsk

SEA   OF   OKHOTSK

Ust'-Bol'sheretsk

Tura

Vilyuysk

Yakutsk

Amga

Aldan

Nel'kan

DZHUGDZHUR KHREBET

Ayan

SHANTAR

SAKHALIN
(Sov. Union)

Aleksandrovsk

Baykit

Podkamennaya Tunguska

Mukhtuya

Olekminsk

Aldan

Tommot

Chumikan

Uda

Poronaysk

Uglegorsk

M. TERPENIYA

E

Yartsevo

G. Polkan
3543

Peleduy

Vitim

Golets
Purpula
2377

PATOM
PLATEAU

Golets
Skalistyy
9186

Tyndinskiy

Zeya

Nikolayevsk-na-Amure

Komsomol'sk-
na-Amure

Sovetskaya
Gavan'

Kholmsk

Yuzhno-Sakhalinsk

Korsakov

Yeniseysk

Bodaybo

STANOVOY KHREBET

Skovorodino

Svobodnyy

Belogorsk

Ust'-Tyrma

Wakkanai

HOKKAIDŌ

Otaru   Sapporo

Kirensk

Nizhne-Angarsk

BURYAT

Zeya

Birobidzhan

Khabarovsk

Esashi

KHREBET BUREINSKIY

Ilimsk

Zhigolovo

Kachuga

Baykal
Lake Baikal
Surface 1535 ft.
above sea level

KHREBET

Nerchinsk

Chita

Sretensk

NERCHINSKIY KHREBET

Blagoveshchensk

Nenjiang

Goukou

Dolnerechensk

Spassk-
Dal'niy

Ussuriysk

LESSER
KHINGAN
RANGE

Bol'

SIKHOTE ALIN'

KHREBET

N

NETSK   Krasnoyarsk

Bogotol

Balakhta

Kansk   Tayshet   Bratsk

Nizhneudinsk

Tulun

Bratskoye
Vdkhr.

Barguzin

Ulan-Ude

Aginskoye

Borzya

GREATER
KHINGAN
RANGE

Haifun

Suhua

Boli

Mudanjiang

Ol'ga

Port Arthur

HARBIN

Ar'yev

Artëm

Vladivostok

Nakhodka

Kuznetski

Nizhnedinsk

Piramida
10,801

Zhigolovo

Angarsk

BAYKAL'SKIY KHREBET

Petrovsk-Zabaykal'skiy

YABLONOVYY KHREBET

Aksha

Wenquan

Nenjiang

Qiqihar

Fuyu

Mudanjiang

MANCHURIA

Jilin

Spassk-
Dal'niy

O'lga

Najin

Chŏngjin

SEA   OF   JAPAN

Minusinsk

Abakan

SAYAN

KHREBET

Cheremkhovo

Munku
Sardyk
11457

Irkutsk

Khamar-Daban

Chikoy

Khentei

Tao an

Jarud Qi

CHANGCHUN

Shuangliao

Dunhua

Hunjiang

P'yongyang

NORTH
KOREA

HONSHŪ

Kanazawa

Kyzyl

TANNU-OLA

Ulug
Nuur

Kosogol
Dalai

Selenge Gol

Ulan Bator
(Ulaanbaatar)

Ondorhaan

Kerulen

Wenquan

GREATER KHINGAN RANGE

CHANGCHUN

FUSHUN

SHENYANG

Tottori

Matsue   KOBE

OSAKA

Hiroshima   Okayama   Kōchi

ALTAI   MTS.

Hara Usa

Hovd

Uliastay

HANGAYN NURUU
(KHANGAI) MTS.

Bost Bogd
13,419

Sayr Usa

MONGOLIA

GOBI   OR   SHAMO
(DESERT)

CHINA

Chifeng

Weichang

Chengde

SEOUL

Kaesŏng

SOUTH
KOREA

Taegu

Andong

Matsue

KYOTO

Osaka

Kōchi

Hami

Zhangjiakou

Fengzhen

PEKING
(Beijing)

Baoding

TIANJIN

Lushun

Lüda

Bo
Hai

SHANDONG
BANDAO

Korea Bay

P'yongyang

YELLOW
SEA

PUSAN

Korea Strait

F

90°   10   Longitude East 100° of Greenwich   11   110°   12   13   14

0   100   200   300   400   500   600 Miles
0   200   400   600   800   1000 Kilometers

COPYRIGHT BY
RAND McNALLY & COMPANY
MADE IN U.S.A.

Asia · *Terrain*

Asia is the largest continent. It covers more area than North America, Europe, and Australia combined. Because it is so big, it is a land of many extremes. It has some of the world's highest mountains, longest rivers, largest deserts, and coldest and hottest climates.

Asia begins at the Ural Mountains in the Soviet Union and extends more than three thousand miles (almost five thousand kilometers), all the way to the Pacific Ocean. This northern region is part of the Soviet Union and is known as Siberia. It is a mostly cold and barren area that is covered with ice and snow for half of the year. Few people live here.

To the south of Siberia is an equally large, equally harsh region. This area begins in the deserts of Saudi Arabia and sweeps across central Asia through Jordan, Iraq, Iran, into the Soviet Union, through parts of China, and on into the deserts of Mongolia. Because of the poor climate and soil, not many people live here, either.

This area is bounded in the south by the highest mountains on the earth, the Himalayas. The two peaks that are considered the highest in the world, Mount Everest and K2, are in the Himalayas.

South of the Himalayas is a warm, wet triangle of land that contains India, Pakistan, Bangladesh, and a couple of smaller nations. Here the climate is friendlier and the land more fertile, so many people live in this area. In fact, this is one of the world's most crowded regions. Several important rivers are found in here, including the Indus, the Ganges, and the Brahmaputra.

Summer *monsoons*, or rain-bearing winds, sweep across India from June to September. The monsoons blow from the southwest, across the Indian Ocean, picking up moisture and carrying rain to India and part of Pakistan. The monsoons make the difference between good and bad crops.

To the east lies Southeast Asia, a land that is a giant rain forest. It is very fertile and has plenty of rainfall. These factors make Southeast Asia a good place to live, so the countries of this region are highly populated. There are several important rivers here, and many, many islands off the mainland. Indonesia is a nation made up exclusively of islands.

North of Southeast Asia is an

Farmers grow rice on the hilly terrain of Nepal by planting it in terraced fields. The Himalayas are in the background.

Crops in Israel's Negev Desert are *irrigated,* or supplied with pumped water.

©1988, 1979 Rand McNally & Co.

Asia Facts
Largest continent
First in population: 3,074,900,000
104 metropolitan areas with over
    1 million population
World's highest mountain: Everest,
    29,028 feet (8,848 meters)
World's largest "lake": Caspian Sea,
    143,240 square miles (371,000
    square kilometers)
World's lowest inland point: Dead Sea,
    1,319 feet (402 meters) below sea
    level

area known as the Far East. It includes most of China, North Korea, South Korea, and Japan. Many people live in these countries. More people live in China than in any other country of the world.

China has three major rivers. In the north is the Huang (Yellow). The Yangtze is in the south, and so is the Xi. Many people have settled along these rivers.

The four main Japanese islands are part of a chain of recently formed volcanic mountains. Much of the land is covered with ash and lava.

Asia · *Animals*

Asia spreads from far northern lands that are covered with snow nine months a year to steamy, hot, southern jungles. Thus, an enormous number of different kinds of animals are found here.

Reindeer, foxes, hare, and tiny, mouselike lemmings live in northern Asia. In northern China and Korea lives the thick-furred Siberian tiger, completely at home in cold and snow. The biggest of all cats, it is often as much as thirteen feet (about four meters) long.

In the cold deserts of central Asia is the two-humped Bactrian camel. The Bactrian camel's relative, the one-humped Arabian camel, or dromedary, is found on warmer deserts to the west. Yaks — huge, furry wild cattle — live in the high, cold land of Tibet, in China. Camels and yaks are tamed by people

and used as beasts of burden.

In the forests of southern Asia live monkeys, leopards, small herds of wild cattle called gaurs, and a few tigers. Indian elephants move through the forests in herds from ten to fifty. Neither as big nor as fierce as African elephants, they are easily tamed, and many have been trained to work for people.

The deadly king cobra, whose bite can kill a human within fifteen minutes, also makes the forest its home. So does the cobra's enemy, the mongoose, which attacks cobras and other kinds of snakes.

In the bamboo forests in the part of Asia where China and Tibet come together lives the giant panda. Although the giant panda and the smaller red panda resemble bears, they are not bears. They are related to the raccoon family.

Imperial Eagle

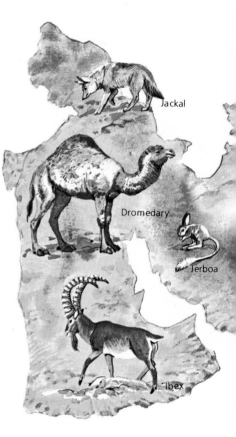

Jackal

Dromedary

Jerboa

Ibex

The largest horns grown by any wild animal are those of a sheep called the Pamir argali, or Marco Polo's argali. Marco Polo saw this animal during his travels across Asia. The sheep's horns spiral outward and sometimes reach lengths of seventy-five inches (almost two hundred centimeters).

Polar Bear

Killer Whale

Arctic Fox

Willow Grouse

Sea Eagle

Elk

Snowy Owl

Wolf

Lynx

Przewalski's Horse

Harbor Seal

Saiga

Raccoon-like Dog

Japanese Macaque

Yak

Giant Panda

Bactrian Camel

Mandarin Duck

Japanese Crane

Snow Leopard

Pheasant

Indian Elephant

Water Buffalo

Dolphin

Tiger

Cormorant

Flyingfish

Macaque

Peafowl

Gibbon

Cobra

Orangutan

Mongoose

Asia · *Life on the Land*

More than half the people in the world live in Asia, and about two-thirds of them make their living by farming. Throughout the world, people tend to live in areas where the climate and land are good for farming. These areas in Asia are quite crowded.

In much of China, Japan, India, and warm, wet Southeast Asia, rice is the most important crop. It is the main food of many Asian people, and Asia produces most of the world's rice.

Cotton is the main crop of parts of southwestern Asia, or the Middle East. Coffee, olives, grapes, dates, citrus fruits, and grains are also raised.

The land of northern Asia is too cold for much farming. And the soil in central Asia is not good for growing crops. In these regions, some people raise reindeer, cattle, and sheep.

Petroleum, or oil, is one of the most important substances in the world today. It is used as fuel, and it is used in many manufactured products. The deserts of the Middle East contain much oil. The countries of this region sell oil to many other countries around the world. More than one-half of all the world's oil comes from this part of Asia.

There is not much industry in most of Asia, but there is a lot in Israel, China, and the eastern Soviet Union. Industry in South Korea, Taiwan, Singapore, and Hong Kong is growing rapidly. And Japan is a world leader in manufacturing.

The Arabs of the Middle East tell a story about a young boy named Aladdin, who finds an old lamp. He rubs the lamp and a genie appears to grant his wishes.

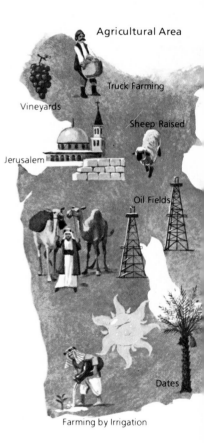

Agricultural Area

Truck Farming

Vineyards

Sheep Raised

Jerusalem

Oil Fields

Dates

Farming by Irrigation

The Indonesian island of Bali, off of Southeast Asia, is known for its folk dances. One, called the *legong*, tells an ancient story of love and battle. Each movement has a meaning and tells part of the story.

Mining

Fur Trapping

Logging

Truck Farming

Reindeer Herds

Mining

Rice Grown

Smelting of Ore

Mining

Truck Farming

Cossack Dancer

Logging

Light and Heavy Industry

Wheatlands

Great Wall of China

Wheatlands

Tea Grown

Hydroelectric Power

Citrus Fruits Grown

Sheep Raised

Gate of Heavenly Peace

Steel Manufactured

Goods Shipped by Caravan

Smelting of Ore

Farming

Chinese Junk

Ruins of Persepolis, Persia

Palace of the Dalai Lama

Traditional Chinese Urn

Agricultural Area

Agricultural Area

Persian Carpet

Corn

Manufacturing

Cacao (Chocolate)

Wheat

Cotton

Mt. Everest

Coconuts

Taj Mahal

Bathing in the Sacred Ganges

Burmese Temples

Fishing

Logging

Rice Grown

Tea Grown

Oil

Coconuts

Agricultural Area

Rubber

Fishing

Teak

Coffee

Asia · *Countries and Cities*

As a result of many kinds of disagreements, Asia has been the site of several recent wars. In the 1980s, the Soviet Union has been fighting in Afghanistan, Iran and Iraq have been at war, and there has been civil war in Lebanon. Other disagreements have been going on for decades. The borders of Israel, for example, have been in dispute since the country was founded in 1948. In India, different religious and ethnic groups have been battling for power for many years.

In the 1970s, the names of a few Asian countries changed. North and South Vietnam became a united country called simply Vietnam. East Pakistan became Bangladesh, and Cambodia became Kampuchea.

The nations of Asia have different kinds of governments. In Israel, the people elect their leaders. In some countries, the military has taken control. Communist governments rule China, the Soviet Union, and a few other countries. A king governs Saudi Arabia. Rulers called *sheikhs* control Bahrain, Qatar, and the United Arab Emirates.

© 1988, 1979 Rand McNally & Co.

Built to keep out invaders, the Great Wall of China is over 1,500 miles (almost 2,500 kilometers) long. It is so big and long, it can be seen from the moon. Parts of the wall are more than two thousand years old.

The people of different parts of Asia are very different, and so are their languages. About one billion people live in China. They speak different types of Chinese, with Mandarin the most common dialect. Hindi, the language of India, is spoken by many people in that country. Indians also speak about one thousand other dialects. Many Indians cannot understand one another's language. Arabic is spoken in many countries of the Middle East, and Russian is spoken by many people in the Soviet Union. Most of the other countries of Asia have their own languages. Many Asian languages have their own alphabet, so they not only sound different from each other, but they also look different.

Some of the oldest cities on earth are in Asia. It is believed that the first cities began in what is now Iraq. There were also cities in India and China in ancient times. Today, many cities in the Middle East have very long histories. Jerusalem, in Israel, is a very old city that has long been an important religious center.

Some of the cities of Asia are very large. It is no surprise that China, with the largest population of any country in the world, has two of the biggest cities in the world: Peking and Shanghai. India, second in the world in population, also has several large cities. Japan is a much smaller country than China or India, but Tokyo, Japan, and its neighbor, Yokohama, contain more people than any other urban area in the world.

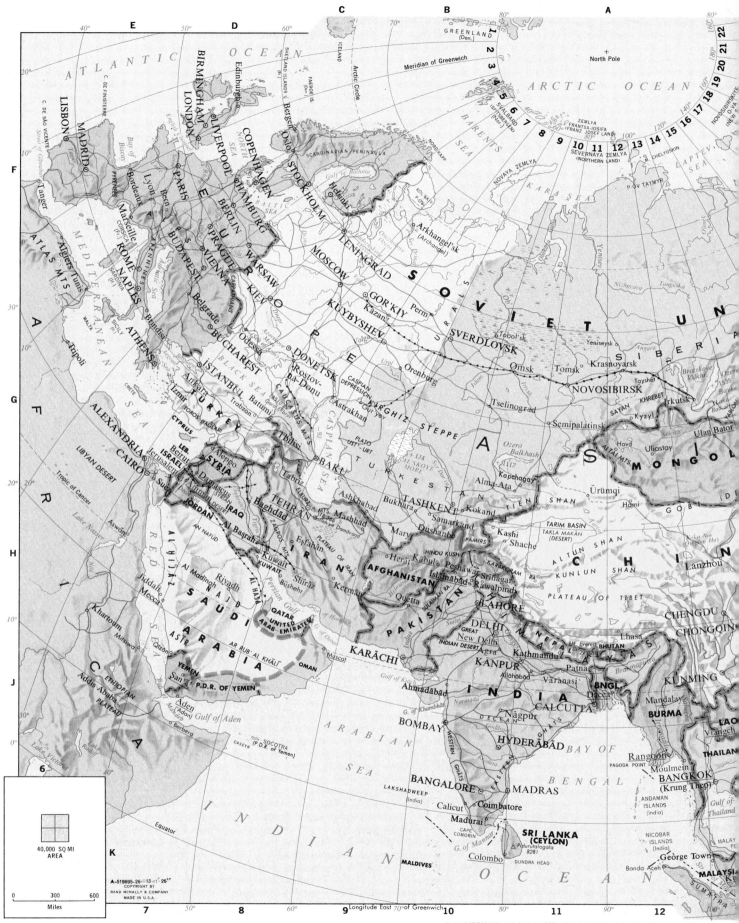

Scale 1:42,000,000; one inch to 665 miles. Lambert's Azimuthal, Equal Area Projection
Elevations and depressions are given in feet

40,000 SQ MI
AREA

0   300   600
Miles

A-519695-26-13-11-26
COPYRIGHT BY
RAND MCNALLY & COMPANY
MADE IN U.S.A.

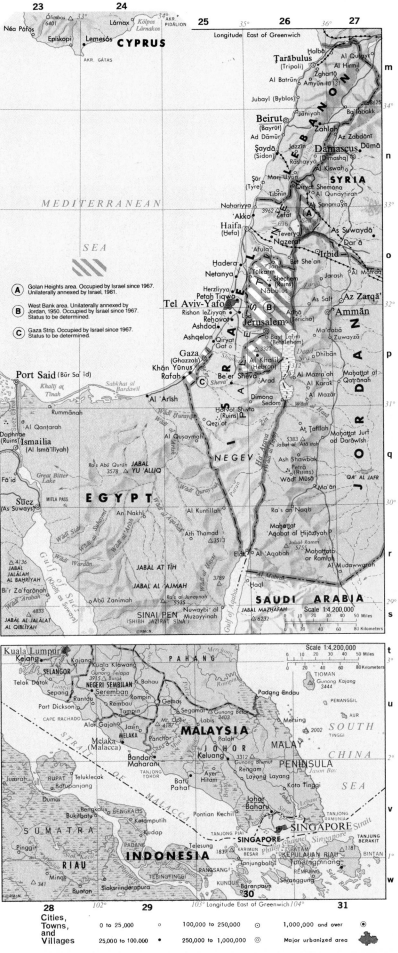

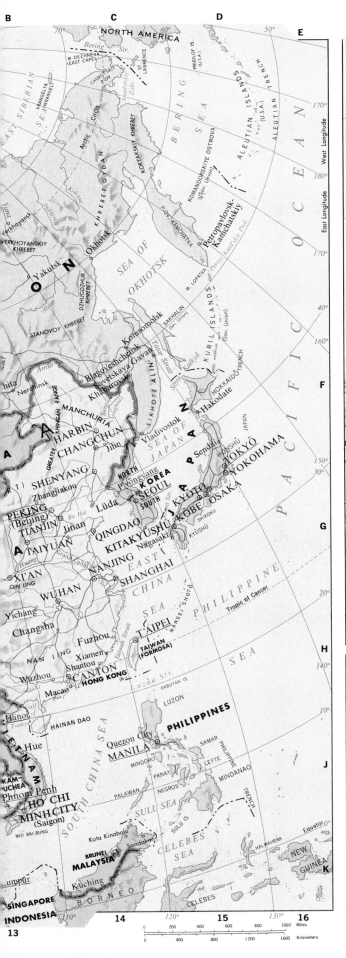

Africa · *Terrain*

The continent of Africa is second in size only to Asia. Yet it seems that few people realize just how huge it is. The entire United States could be placed in just the Sahara Desert, which extends 3,200 miles (5,150 kilometers) across northern Africa.

Africa is a gigantic plateau that stands well above sea level. It is mostly lower in the north and west and higher in the east and south. On all sides, the edges drop off abruptly into the surrounding oceans and seas.

Many people think Africa is a land of jungles. In reality, most of Africa is covered with either desert or grassland. The Sahara takes up most of northern Africa. The Kalahari and Namib deserts lie in southern Africa. Between the two desert regions are many, many miles of grassland called *savanna*. Only the middle of Africa, the land of the Congo River, is jungle.

Africa has some magnificent mountains. The Atlas Mountains form a major chain at the top of the continent, through Morocco, Algeria, and Tunisia. These mountains were formed at the same time as the Alps of Europe. Both mountain ranges are the result of the collision of Africa with Europe many millions of years ago. After the collision, Africa drifted back south. The gap between the two continents filled with water to become the Mediterranean Sea. Many mountain ranges are the

Victoria Falls is on the Zambezi River in southern Africa. It is over a mile (about one and a half kilometers) wide, and it drops nearly four hundred feet (about 120 meters). It is bigger than Niagara Falls.

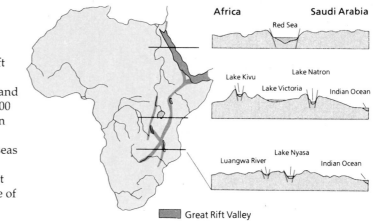

Africa's Great Rift Valley extends about four thousand miles (almost 6,500 kilometers). It can be traced by the many lakes and seas that fill parts of it. The cutaway at right shows some of those bodies of water.

Great Rift Valley

result of collisions such as the one between Africa and Europe.

In East Africa, there are two rows of mountains. Mount Kilimanjaro, Africa's highest peak, is in the eastern row.

Between the peaks lies the Great Rift Valley. This is a long rip in the earth's surface where the land dropped down more

than a mile (about one and a half kilometers). Several beautiful lakes are in this rift, including Lake Victoria, which is almost as big as Scotland.

The Drakensberg Mountains in southern Africa are the most unusual range on the continent. Actually, they are not true mountains, just tilted-up por-

Africa Facts
Second largest continent
Third in population: 617,500,000
25 metropolitan areas with over
    1 million population
Highest mountain: Kilimanjaro, 19,340
    feet (5,895 meters)
World's largest desert: Sahara,
    approximately 3,500,000 square
    miles (9,065,000 square kilometers)
World's longest river system: Nile, 4,145
    miles (6,650 kilometers)
World's highest recorded temperature:
    Azizia, Libya, 136°F (58°C)
Equator passes through

tions of the gigantic plateau that makes up Africa.

Four important rivers flow out of Africa. The Niger runs through several West African countries and out into the Atlantic Ocean. The Congo flows west out of central Africa. The Zambezi, toward southern Africa, flows east to the Indian Ocean. And finally, the Nile flows northward through several countries, including Egypt, and empties into the Mediterranean Sea. The Nile is the longest river in the world.

Deserts such as this one in Egypt cover much of North Africa. Yet people have managed to live here for thousands of years. Camels do not need water often, so people use them as beasts of burden. An ancient pyramid looms in the background.

Africa · *Animals*

Africa is a continent of jungles, grassy plains, and deserts. Each kind of land has different types of animals that have adapted to the living conditions. Many African animals are beautiful, wondrous creatures. But many of these magnificent beasts are in danger of becoming extinct because people hunt them and because people want to use the land on which the animals live.

In North Africa, the huge Sahara Desert spreads across thousands of miles. Not many animals can live in a desert, and those that do are able to survive with little or no water. In places where plants grow, there are a few herds of addax, a little antelope with twisted horns. An addax never drinks. It gets the moisture it needs from the plants it eats. The best-known animal of the Sahara is the one-humped Arabian camel. These animals were brought to the Sahara by people, and all camels in the Sahara are used as tame beasts of burden.

In the forests of central Africa live the chimpanzee and gorilla. Here, too, are buffalo, leopards, and many kinds of birds and monkeys. In the swamps and rivers are crocodiles and hippopotamuses.

In the vast, grassy plains that lie north and south of the central rain forests are many of the best-known animals of Africa. Herds of zebra, eland, and gnu, or wildebeest, graze on these plains. Giraffes and rhinoceroses feed on plants. African elephants, the largest of all land animals, and cheetahs, the fastest of all animals, roam the plains. The plains are also home to the African lion.

Gorillas are peaceful animals that live in the central African jungle. Like many of the great beasts of Africa, gorillas are in danger of becoming extinct.

Africa · *Life on the Land*

Some Africans carve ceremonial masks by hand, as they have for centuries. This mask is too large to wear. It is probably a decoration.

Agricultural Area

Peanuts

Chocolate

Most Africans are either farmers or herders. Many of them live as their ancestors did for thousands of years. They roam the land for food or live in tiny villages, raising crops and animals, usually not to sell to other countries, but for their own use.

Little farming can be done in hot, dry North Africa. But along the coasts of Morocco, Algeria, and Tunisia, farmers can grow a few crops. About half the people of Egypt work farmlands along the banks of the Nile, mainly growing cotton. Mining for oil is important in Algeria and Libya.

West Africa is an important agricultural area. Among other crops, people here grow cacao beans, from which chocolate and cocoa are made. The forests of central Africa produce rubber trees and banana trees. In East Africa, herding cattle has been the main way of life for many years.

The Kalahari Desert covers thousands of square miles of southern Africa. It is the home of some of the world's last Stone Age people, who hunt and gather whatever food they can find.

But farther south, in the country of South Africa, the fertile land is farmed by the descendants of Europeans who settled there many years ago. The land of South Africa also has many minerals. Most of the world's diamonds and gold come from famous mines in that country. South Africa is the only African nation in which much manufacturing is done.

A famous African tale tells of Ananse the Spider Man, who tried to keep all the wisdom in the world for himself by stuffing it in a large pot. But the pot fell as Ananse tried to hide it in a tree, and all the wisdom blew away.

Agricultural Area

Moorish-style Architecture

Corn

Wheat

Vineyards

Olives

Oil Fields

Nomad with Goats

Goods Shipped by Caravan

Fishing

Tobacco

Cairo

Sphinx

The Great Pyramid at Giza

Dates Harvested

Cotton Grown

Cotton Made into Cloth

Sand Dunes

African Village

Leather Products Made

Sheep Raised

Rubber

Palm Oil

Mining

Cattle Raised

Plantains (African Bananas)

Tourists Welcomed

Cattle Raised

Cacao Beans (Chocolate)

Central Forests

Copra (Dried Coconut) Shipped

Oil Fields

Pygmy

Mt. Kilimanjaro

Minerals Mined

Agricultural Area

Masai Tribesman

Corn

Coal Mines

Tea

Victoria Falls

Diamond Mines

Citrus Fruits

Yams

Vanilla Beans Grown

Sheep Raised

Gold Mines

Africa • *Countries and Cities*

By the 1400s, Europeans began sailing to Africa and conquering the peoples who lived there. The Europeans were interested mainly in profiting from the vast resources they found in Africa.

By the early 1900s, almost all of Africa was under European rule. The borders of many African countries were set up by Europeans who settled there. Most of the European govern-

ments are gone now, but the boundaries they set up still exist.

Since the Europeans have left, most African countries have become *independent*, meaning

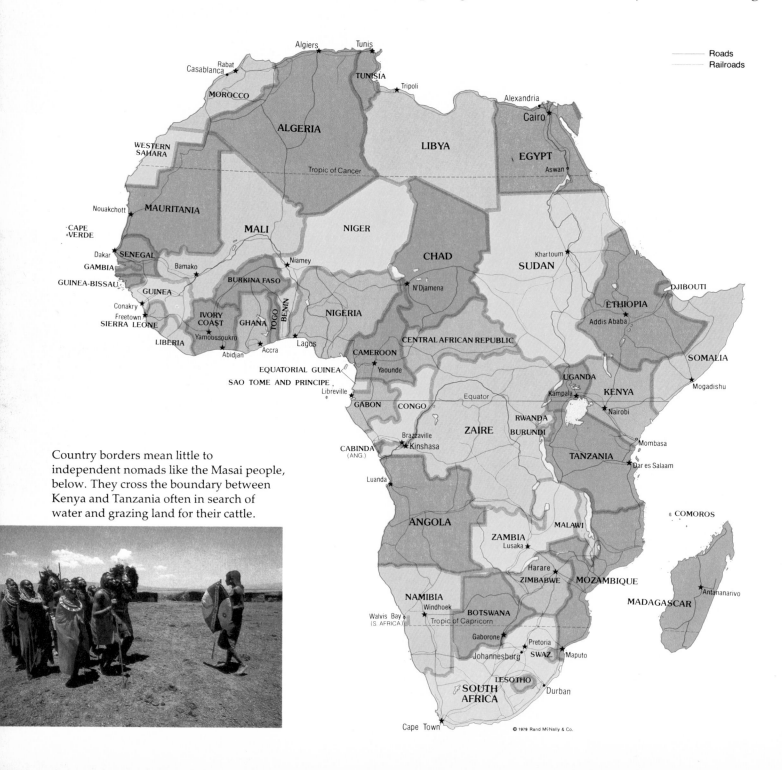

Country borders mean little to independent nomads like the Masai people, below. They cross the boundary between Kenya and Tanzania often in search of water and grazing land for their cattle.

© 1979 Rand McNally & Co.

that they rule themselves. Most are ruled by African leaders. In some countries, military leaders have taken control. In others, a dominant political party is in control.

Very often, observers group the countries of Africa into large regions that have things in common, such as the types of people that live there and the languages they speak. Many of the people of North Africa are Arabs who speak Arabic and practice the Muslim religion. These people have a very long history. Egypt was the site of one of the first cultures on earth. Some of the cities of Egypt, including Alexandria and Cairo, are very old and have many beautiful old buildings. Cairo is also the biggest city in Africa.

West Africa is heavily populated with black Africans. Favorable conditions for farming and access to the ocean help make this region a good place to live. One-fourth of all people in Africa live in the countries that border the Atlantic Ocean. Nigeria has the biggest population of all African countries. The people of West Africa are composed of many different ethnic groups, and each group has its own languages.

The equator passes through another region, central Africa. Zaire is the biggest country here. Again, different groups of black Africans live in this area, and the groups have their own languages.

East Africa is separated from the rest of the continent by mountains and the Great Rift Valley. Here are grasslands on

Less than one third of the African population lives in cities, making Africa the least *urbanized* continent. Very often, the capital is the only city of any great size in a country. Such is the case with Nairobi, Kenya, shown above.

These women are carrying their wares to market as their ancestors did before them. Colorful cotton cloth has been made in the West African country of Nigeria for centuries.

which groups of people herd cattle and many wild animals roam. Kenya and Tanzania have set aside vast areas where the animals are protected from hunters. Nairobi, the capital of Kenya, is a modern city that is growing in population.

Less than 20 percent of the population of the country of

South Africa is of European descent, but this small group controls the government and most of the wealth of the country. The people of South Africa live in a system called *apartheid*, in which there are very strict controls about separating the blacks, whites, and other groups that live there.

ATLANTIC OCEAN

AÇORES (AZORES) (Port.)
Same scale as main map

GRACIOSA
TERCEIRA
FAIAL
PICO
SÃO JORGE
SÃO MIGUEL
Ponta Delgada
STA. MARIA

SPAIN
Cádiz
Str. of Gibraltar
Gibraltar (U.K.)
Tanger (Tangier)
Larache
Ceuta (Sp.)
Tetouan
Ouezzane
Melilla (Sp.)
Beni Sof
Delles
Algiers (El Djazaïr)
Ech Cheliff
Cherchell
Oran
Mestghanem
Ghilizane
Tizi-Ouzou
Bejaïa (Bougie)
El Coll
Miliana
Stif
El Boulaïda
Skikda
Annaba
Bône
Guelma
Souk Ahras
Tunis
Bizerte
TUNISIA
Sfax

CASABLANCA
Rabat
Salé
Meknès
Fès
Taza
Oujda
Tilimsen
Saïda
El Djelfa
Aflou
Laghouat
Wargla
Touggourt
El Wad
Gabès
Sousse
El Kaïrouan

MOROCCO
Marrakech
Essaouira
Agadir
Taroudant
Demnat
Jebel Toubkal 13665
Azemmour
El Jadida
Settat
Oued-Zem
Kasba-Tadla
Boudenib
Figuig
Béchar
Igli
Béni Abbas
Ghardaïa
El Menia
Hassi Messaoud
Ghudamis
Daraj
Nālūt
AL HAM AL HA

ATLAS MOUNTAINS

ISLAS CANARIAS (Sp.)
LA PALMA
TENERIFE
GOMERA
HIERRO
GRAN CANARIA
San Sebastián
Sta. Cruz de Tenerife
Las Palmas de Gran Canaria
LANZAROTE
FUERTEVENTURA
CAP DRÂA
C. YUBY
Sidi Ifni
Tiznit
ANTI ATLAS
Oued Drâa

ALGERIA
GRAND ERG OCCIDENTAL
GRAND ERG ORIENTAL
PLATEAU DU TADEMAÏT
Adrar
In Salah
Timimoun
Bordj Omar Idriss
In Amnas
PLATEAU DU TINGHERT
TIDIKELT
TASSILI-N-AJJER
Illizi
Sardalas

FUNCHAL
ILHA DE PORTO SANTO
ILHA DA MADEIRA
DA MADEIRA (Port.)
ARQUIPÉLAGO

El Aaiún
CABO BOJADOR
WESTERN SAHARA
The Western Sahara is occupied by Morocco
Tindouf
Chenachane
ERG IGUIDI
ERG CHECH
EL HANK
TANEZROUFT
Ouallene
Ghât
Djanet
AHAGGAR
Tahat 9541
Mt. Grébour 6562

Dakhla
Fdérik
Tropic of Cancer
EL DJOUF
Taoudenni
SAHARA
Oued Tamenghest
Tamenghest
TUAREG
Iferouâne 5906
Monts Tamgak

Nouâdhibou
CAP BLANC
CAP D'ARGUIN
Atar
Chinguetti
OUARANE
EL MREYYÉ
Mabrouk
ADRAR DES IFOGHAS
AÏR
Monts Bagzane 6300

Nouâmrhar
CAP TIMIRIS
Akjoujt
MAURITANIA
Tidjikdja
Araouane
Kidal
Agadez
TÉNÉRÉ

Nouakchott
Boutilimit
Aleg
Kiffa
Néma
Oualâta
Tombouctou (Timbuktu)
Bamba
MALI
NIGER

Saint-Louis
Podor
Dagana
Matam
Kaédi
Mbout
Sélibaby
Linguère
Louga
Bakel
Nioro du Sahel
Nara
Goumbou
Niafounké
Goundam
Bourem
Gao
Tahoua
Tessaoua
Gouré
Ngu

CAP VERT
Rufisque
Dakar
Thiès
Diourbel
SENEGAL
Kaolack
Kayes
Bafoulabé
Ségou
Djenné
San
Mopti
Bandiagara
Tillabéry
Niamey
Dosso
Say
Madaoua
Maradi
Zinder

Banjul (Bathurst)
GAMBIA
Ziguinchor
Casamance
Gambie
Tambacounda
Kita
Koulikoro
Bani
Dédougou
Ouahigouya
Dori
Kaya
BURKINA FASO
Ouagadougou
Fada Ngourma
Malanville
Kandi
Birnin Kebbi
Sokoto
Kaura Namoda
Katsina
Gumel
Hadejia
Gusau
Gaya
Kano
GEIDAM
BORN PLAIN

GUINEA-BISSAU
Bissau
Bolama
Buba
Boké
Koumbia
ARQUIPÉLAGO DOS BIJAGÓS
FOUTA DJALLON
Labé
Siguiri
Bamako
Satadougou
Kankan
Bougouni
Koutiala
Sikasso
Bobo-Dioulasso
Tenkodogo
Gambaga
Sansané-Mango
Natitingou
Kontagora
Zungeru
Zaria
Kainji Reservoir
Bauchi
Gombe

GUINEA
Timbo
Mamou
Kindia
Boffa
Kouroussa
Mont Tamgue 5046
Mont Nimba 5748
Gaoua
Illo
Jebba
Minna
Bida
Kaduna
NIGERIA
Jos

Conakry
Forécariah
Kabala
Makeni
Kissidougou
Beyla
Odienné
Korhogo
Boura
Bouna
Tamale
Yendi
Sokodé
Parakou
Iseyin
Oyo
Ogbomosho
Oshogbo
Ilorin
Baro
Keffi
Lokoja
Makurdi
Idah
Ibi
Yola
ADAMA

SIERRA LEONE
Freetown
Moyamba
Pendembu
Kolahun
Séguéla
Bouaké
Bouaflé
KONG
Kong
Dabakala
Bondoukou
Kintampo
Savalou
Abomey
Ibadan
Iwo
Ife
Ilesha
GHANA
Kumasi
Koforidua
Benin City
Onitsha
Enugu
Katsina Ala
Kontcha
GOTEL MTS.

Bonthe
Bum Hills
Robertsport
Monrovia
Buchanan
River Cess
Greenville
LIBERIA
Yamoussoukro
IVORY COAST
Abidjan
Port-Bouët
Tarkwa
Accra
Lomé
Porto-Novo
Lagos
Sapele
Warri
Owerri
Aba
Port Harcourt
Brass
Bonny 13451
Calabar
Kumba
Mamfe
Dschang
Foumban
CAMERO

CAPE PALMAS
Harper
Tabou
Grand Lahou
Grand Bassam
Assini
C. THREE POINTS
Sekondi-Takoradi
Cape Coast
Saltpond
Keta
Grand Popo
Cotonou
Forcados
Bight of Benin

ATLANTIC OCEAN
GULF OF GUINEA
BIGHT OF BIAFRA

CAPE VERDE
SANTA ANTÃO
SÃO VICENTE
SÃO NICOLAU
SAL
BOA VISTA
SÃO TIAGO
FOGO
MAIO
Praia
Same scale as main map
©RMcN.

ILHA DO PRINCIPE
SÃO TOMÉ AND PRINCIPE
EQUATORIAL GUINEA
Bata
Malabo
BIOKO
RIO MUNI
Kribi
Campo
Edéa
Eséka
Yaoundé
Douala
Libreville
Oyem
Makokou
GABON

ILHA DE SÃO TOMÉ
São Tomé

Longitude West of Greenwich
Longitude East of Greenwich

Cities,
Towns,
and
Villages

0 to 25,000
25,000 to 100,000
100,000 to 250,000
250,000 to 1,000,000
1,000,000 and over
Major urbanized area

Scale 1:16,850,000; one inch to 265 miles. Sinusoidal Projection
Elevations and depressions are given in feet

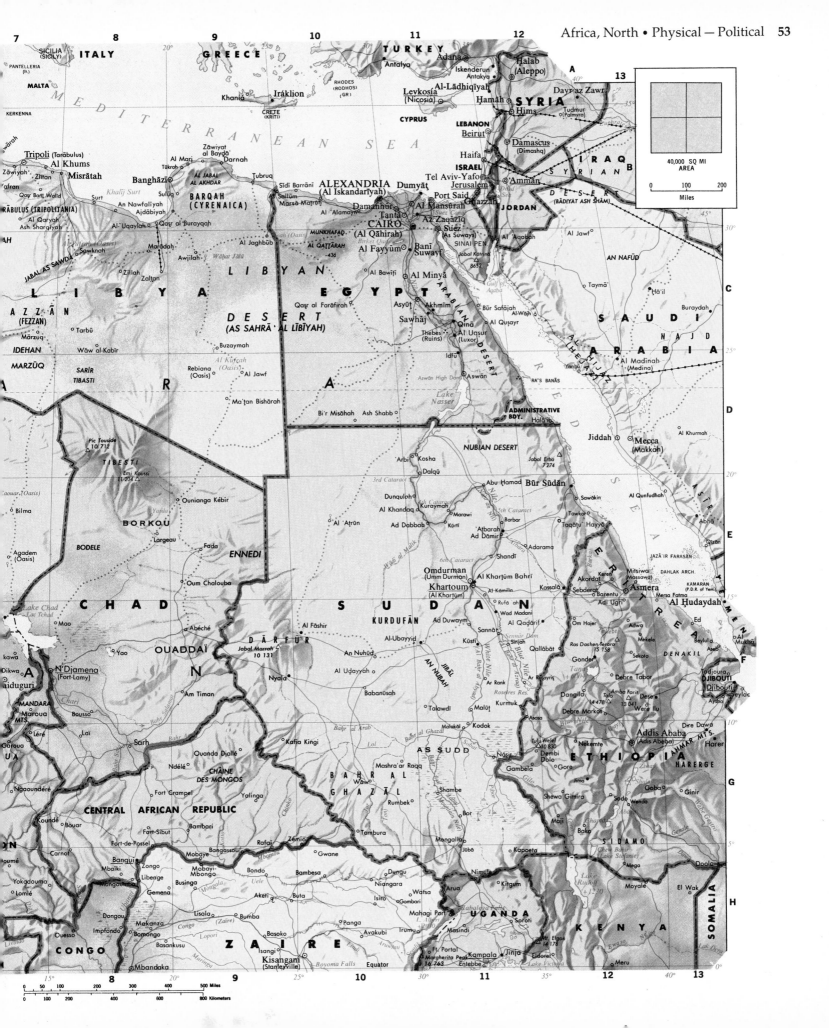

40,000 SQ MI AREA

0   100   200
Miles

MEDITERRANEAN SEA

ITALY
SICILIA (SICILY)
PANTELLERIA (It.)
MALTA
KERKENNA

GREECE
Khaniá
Iráklion
CRETE (KRITI)
RHODES (RODHOS) (GR)

TURKEY
Antalya
Adana
Iskenderun
Antakya
Halab (Aleppo)

SYRIA
Al-Lādhiqīyah
Hamāh
Hims
Dayr az Zawr
Tudmur (Palmyra)

CYPRUS
Levkosía (Nicosia)

LEBANON
Beirut
Damascus (Dimashq)

IRAQ
SYRIAN DESERT (BĀDIYAT ASH SHĀM)

Tripoli (Tarābulus)
Al Khums
Misrātah
Zāwiyah
Zlitan
afran
Qasr Bani Walid
Banghāzī
Tūkrah
Al Marj
Zāwiyat al Baydā
Darnah
Tubruq
Sulūq

BARQAH (CYRENAICA)
AL JABAL AL AKHDAR

Sīdī Barrānī
Sallūm
Marsá Matrūh
Al 'Alamayn

ALEXANDRIA (Al Iskandarīyah)
Dumyāt
Damanhūr
Al Mansūrah
Tantā
Az Zaqāzīq
Port Said

Haifa
Tel Aviv-Yafo
ISRAEL
Jerusalem
Ghazzah
Amman
JORDAN

Al 'Aqabah
Al Jawf

Khalīj Surt
Surt
An Nawfalīyah
Ajdābiyā
Al Qaryah
Ash Sharqīyah
Qasr al Burayqah
Al 'Uqaylah

CAIRO (Al Qāhirah)
Al Fayyūm
Suez (As Suways)
SINAI PEN.
Jabal Katrina 8652

RABULUS (TRIPOLITANIA)

Al Jaghbūb
(Oasis) Siwah
MUNKHAFAD AL QATTĀRAH -436

Banī Suwayf
Al Minyā
Al Bawiti

AN NAFUD

Taymā
Hā'il
Buraydah

AZZĀN (FEZZAN)

JABAL AS SAWDĀ
Sawknah
Marādah
Awjilah
Wāhat Jālū

LIBYAN
DESERT (AS SAHRĀ' AL LĪBĪYAH)

Qasr al Farāfirah
Asyūt
Akhmīm
Sawhāj
Qinā
Al Uqsur (Luxor)
Thebes (Ruins)
Bi'r Safājah
Al Quşayr
Al Wajh

SAUDI
NAJD
ARABIA
Al Madīnah (Medina)

Marzūq
Tarbū
Wāw al-Kabīr

IDEHAN
MARZŪQ

SARĪR TIBASTI

Buzaymah
Al Kufrah (Oasis)
Rebiana (Oasis)
Al Jawf

Idfū
Aswān High Dam
Aswān

RA'S BANĀS

Jiddah
Mecca (Makkah)
Al Khurmah

Ma'tan Bishārah
Bi'r Misāhah
Ash Shabb

Lake Nasser

ADMINISTRATIVE BDY.
Halā'ib

Pic Touside 10 712
TIBESTI
Emi Koussi 11 204

NUBIAN DESERT
Jabal Erba 7 274

3rd Cataract
'Arbi
Kosha
Dalqū

Sawākin
Al Qunfudhah
Abhā

BORKOU
BODELE
Largeau
Fada
ENNEDI
Ounianga Kébir
Yarda
Bilma
Agadem (Oasis)

Dunqulah
4th Cataract
Al Khandaq
Kuraymah
Ad Dabbah
Marawi
Al 'Atrūn
Kūrti
5th Cataract
Atbarah
Ad Dāmir
Barbar

Abu Hamad
Būr Sūdān
Tawkar
Taqatu' Hayyā

JAZĀ'IR FARASĀN
DAHLAK ARCH.
KAMARAN (P.D.R. of Yem.)
Mersa Fatma

Oum Chalouba

Wādi al Malik
6th Cataract
Shandi
Adarama

Akordat
Mitsiwa (Massawa)
Asmera
ERITREA

CHAD
Lake Chad
Lac Tchad
Mao

Omdurman (Umm Durman)
Khartoum (Al Khartūm)
Al Khartūm Bahrī
At Kāmilīn

Kassalā
Sebderat
Barentu
Adi Ugri

Al Hudaydah
YEMEN

OUADDAÏ
Abéché
Yao

DĀRFŪR
Jabal Marrah 10 131
Al Fāshir

SUDAN
KURDUFAN
Rufā'a
Wad Madani
Al Qadārif
Ar Rank

Om Hajer
Adwa
Gonder
Ras Dashen Terara 15 158
Mekele
DENAKIL

Dikwa
N'Djamena (Fort-Lamy)
MANDARA
Maroua
MTS.
Bousso
Léré
Lai

An Nuhūd
Nyala
JIBĀL AN NUBAH
Al 'Ubayyid
Al Uḍayyah
Babanūsah
Kūsti

Sinjah
Sannār
Sennar Dam
Roseires Res.
Qallābāt

Debre Tabor
Tana
Dangila
Tafa
Amba Farit 13 041
Dese
Wera Ilu

Ed
Beylul
Aseb
Al Mukha

Ngaoundéré
Garoua
Sarh

CENTRAL AFRICAN REPUBLIC
Bouar
Koundé
Carnot
Bambari
Fort-Sibut
Fort-de-Possel

CHAÎNE DES MONGOS
Ouanda Djallé
Ndélé
Yalinga

Kafia Kingi
Talawdī
Kurmuk
Malūt

BAHR AL GHAZĀL
Wāw
Mashra'ar Raqq
Rumbek
Shambe

AS SUDD

Dangila 14 478
Debre Markos
Addis Ababa (Adis Abeba)

Nekemte
Dembi Dolo
Gambela
Gore
Jima

Dire Dawa
Harer
HARERGE
ETHIOPIA
AHMAR MTS.

Banqui
Mbaïki
Zongo
Mobaye
Bangassou
Rafai
Zémio
Gwane

Bor
Juba
Mongalla
Nasir

Maji
Bako

Goba
Ginir
SIDAMO

Yokaduma
Lomié
Mongoumba
Libenge
Gemena
Businga
Bondo
Bambesa
Dungu
Niangara

Kapoeta
Nimule
Arua
Kitgum

Chew Bahir
Lake Stefanie
Mega
SOMALIA
Doolow
El Wak

Ouesso
Impfondo
Makanza
Dongou
Lisala
Bumba
Aketi
Buta
Isiro
Gombari
Watsa
Masindi
Soroti

Lake Rudolf +1230
Moyale

CONGO
Bomongo
Basankusu
Basoko
Kisangani (Stanleyville)
Boyoma Falls
Panga
Avakubi
Irumu
L. Albert
Mahagi Port
Nabalega Falls

UGANDA
KENYA
Mbandaka
ZAÏRE
Kampala
Entebbe
Jinja
Lake Victoria
Meru
Eldoret
Mt. Elgon 14 178
Ft. Portal
Margherita Peak 16 763
Equator

The "Homelands" (Bophuthatswana, Ciskei, Transkei, Venda) were unilaterally created by South Africa and are not internationally recognized.

1 Bophuthatswana
2 Ciskei
3 Transkei
4 Venda

CAPE TOWN

Scale 1:1,050,000

0   5   10 Miles
0   4   8   12   16 Kilometers

®RMcN.

Scale 1:16,850,000 ; one inch to 265 miles. Sinusoidal Projection
Elevations and depressions are given in feet

0   50   100   200   300   400   500 Miles
0   100   200   400   600   800 Kilometers

Australia, New Zealand, and Oceania • *Terrain*

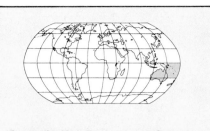

On a map of the world, you can see how big the Pacific Ocean is. It covers more than one-third of the earth's surface. You can also see that the ocean is full of islands of different sizes. No one knows how many islands there are, but people have estimated that there are twenty to thirty thousand. In this part of the world are Australia, New Zealand, and the islands known as Oceania.

Some of the islands of Oceania are the tips of volcanoes that push up above the water. Others are *atolls*, rings of coral surrounding lagoons that remain where volcanoes have sunk back into the ocean. Observers group the islands into three regions. Polynesia includes Hawaii, Samoa, Tahiti, and Easter Island. Micronesia contains the Marshall, Caroline, and Gilbert islands. Melanesia includes

Australia, New Zealand, and Oceania Facts

Australia
Smallest continent
Population: 16,330,000
Highest mountain: Kosciusko,
7,310 feet (2,228 meters)

New Zealand
Two main islands, North Island and
South Island
Population: 3,350,000

Oceania (not including Australia and
New Zealand)
20,000 islands – more or less –
scattered throughout the Pacific
Population: 5,820,000

The mountains of New Zealand's North Island give way in the southwest to hills and then to raised beaches.

Two of Fiji's eight hundred islands in the South Pacific are large, with lovely tree-lined beaches. Most of the others are merely piles of sand on coral reefs.

Ayers Rock towers 1,100 feet (335.28 meters) above the flat Australian desert.

the Fiji Islands and New Guinea.

Australia is the smallest continent. Its main mountain range is known as the Great Dividing Range, and it is near the eastern coast. In the south, this range dips into the sea and rises up again to form Tasmania. The Great Dividing Range is very old, and the mountains have been worn down by water and wind over hundreds of millions of years.

Air moving inland from the Tasman Sea is blocked by the Great Dividing Range and is forced upward. As it rises, it cools and drops rain along the coast. Plenty of rain and the fertile soils of southeastern Australia make this the continent's main agricultural area.

West of the Great Dividing Range is a great desert region. Australians call it the Outback. The mountains keep clouds and rain from moving into the Outback. Part of the Outback is bush country, where some trees and plants grow. The rest of the Outback is made up of three deserts: the Great Sandy, the Gibson, and the Great Victoria. The southwestern coast has low mountains called the Darling Range. Again, these mountains prevent rain clouds from moving inland, but the coastal area is fertile.

Very different from the rest of Australia is Cape York Peninsula. Heat and rain combine to make ideal conditions for the tropical jungles that are found here.

One of the most famous regions of Australia is not on the land, but in the ocean off the northeastern coast. It is called the Great Barrier Reef. It is made up of colorful coral formations and is the home of many sea creatures. It is the largest coral reef in the world.

Two main islands make up New Zealand: North Island and South Island. Both islands have plenty of mountains. On the southwest coast of South Island, long fjords cut into the land, just like the fjords of Norway. On the eastern shore are the flattest plains found in New Zealand.

North Island contains a volcanic region around Lake Taupo. Here there are geysers and pools of steaming mud. This area is a reminder of the activity under the earth's surface that formed the spectacular surrounding mountains.

Australia, New Zealand, and Oceania · *Animals*

Many of the animals of Australia are very different from those in other places. Australia was separated from all other parts of the world for about 50 million years, so its animals evolved in a different way. Most Australian mammals — furry, warm-blooded animals — are *marsupials*. Marsupials are animals like the kangaroo whose babies are kept in a pouch on the mother's body until they are old enough to care for themselves.

Two of the strangest Australian animals are the spiny ant-eater and the duck-billed platypus. They are mammals, but their babies hatch out of eggs, like birds or reptiles. These two creatures may be much like the first kinds of mammals, which lived many millions of years ago.

On the plains of Australia, several kinds of marsupials make their homes. Kangaroos live in little herds and eat grass. Some kangaroos can be as much as seven feet (over two meters) tall, but there are also small kangaroos called wallabies. Wombats look like beavers without tails. They dig tunnels that they sleep in during the day, and they come out at night. Bandicoots live much the same way as wombats.

In the eastern part of Australia lives the koala. Koalas look like little bears, but they are not bears. They are marsupials, and they carry their babies in pouches.

New Zealand does not have many animals that have not been brought by people. But on some islands near New Zealand live little reptiles called tuataras. They are the descendants of reptiles that lived before the dinosaurs. They are the only creatures of their kind anywhere in the world. On the islands of Oceania are found many different kinds of birds and a few marsupials.

Great numbers of sea creatures drift gracefully among the coral reefs — and in the deeper tropical waters — surrounding the islands of Oceania. A few are frightening. Most are brilliantly colored and very beautiful.

Black Marlin

Triggerfish

Butterfly Fish

Emu

Frilled Lizard

Dingo

Cockatoo

Cassowary

Death Adder

Echidna

Tree Kangaroo

Rabbit

Rock Wallaby

Wombat

Great Gray Kangaroo

Kookaburra

Red Kangaroo

Koala

Platypus

Wandering Albatross

White Shark

Slender-billed Shearwater

Black Swan

The koala looks like a soft, cuddly teddy bear. Small, it weighs less than eighteen pounds (8.16 kilograms) when grown. For six months the cub rides in the mother's pouch. Later it rides on her back, even when she climbs high into the eucalyptus trees for the buds and leaves that are the koala's only food.

Dovey Petrel

Kiwi

Tuatara

Kea

Australia, New Zealand, and Oceania · *Life on the Land*

Lumbering

Rain Forest

Water Sports

Sheep Raising

Lumbering

Water Conservation

Uranium Prospecting

Great Barrier Reef

Aborigines in the Outback

Cattle Raising

Mining

Agricultural Area

Sheep Raising

Ayers Rock

Rugby

Going to School by Radio

Mining

Opals Mined

Sydney—Opera House

Lifeguard Teams

Minerals Mined

Citrus Groves

Agricultural Area

Agricultural Area

Water Sports

Wheatlands

Freighter

Fishing

Fruit Grown

Minerals Exported

Maori Carving

Sheep Raising

During the Age of Discovery, Europeans traveled to Australia, New Zealand, and some of the islands of Oceania. They settled the lands they found, and many descendants of Europeans remain on those lands. In Australia, these people have built many businesses, factories, and farms, and today Australia is highly industrialized.

Some people live on the outer edge of the Outback. These people are mostly farmers who raise sheep and cattle.

New Zealand is not as industrialized as Australia, but some manufacturing is done. The raising of sheep and cattle is very important in New Zealand.

In Australia, New Zealand, and neighboring islands, there remain groups of people who have lived here much longer than Europeans have. In Australia there are people known as aborigines, and in New Zealand are the Maoris. Many of these people have adopted modern life-styles.

Australia, New Zealand, and Oceania • *Countries and Cities*

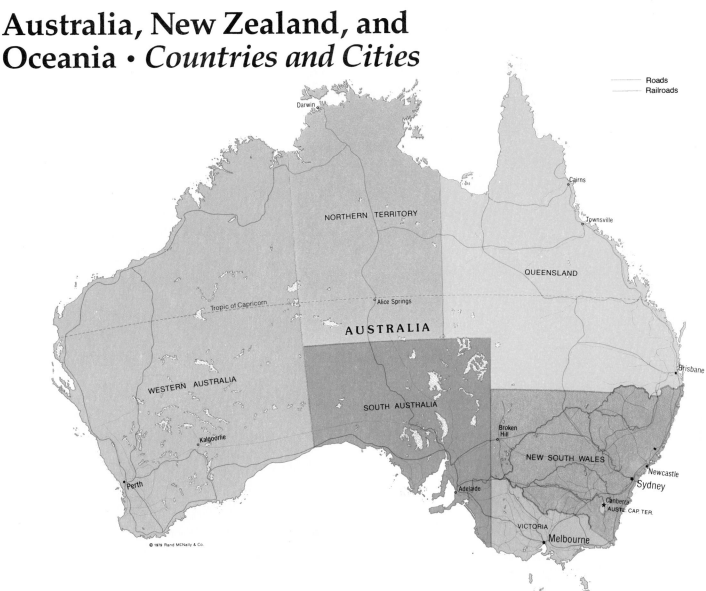

Roads
Railroads

The Land Down Under — that's what Australia and New Zealand are often called. The nickname grew out of the idea that these lands are directly opposite, under the feet of, Europeans.

If you look at a map of the world, you can see that in Australia, to go north is to head for the equator, where the land is closer to the sun, and it is warmer. To go south is to travel toward cold weather.

Australia is the only country that is also a continent. The nation is divided into states, and the people elect their leaders. New Zealand operates the same way. Some of the islands of Oceania are governed by other, bigger countries. Some of them are independent; that is, they govern themselves.

The descendants of Europeans who live in Australia and New Zealand speak English. There are groups of people in these places and on the surrounding islands who have lived there since ancient times, and most of them speak English as well as the languages of their ancestors.

40,000 SQ MI
AREA

0   100   200
Miles

A-590200-26-   -4-5-13
COPYRIGHT BY
RAND MCNALLY & COMPANY
MADE IN U.S.A.

Longitude East of Greenwich

Cities
and
Towns

0 to 50,000   500,000 to 1,000,000

50,000 to 500,000   1,000,000 and over

Scale 1:16,850,000 ; one inch to 265 miles. Lambert's Azimuthal, Equal Area Projection

Elevations and depressions are given in feet

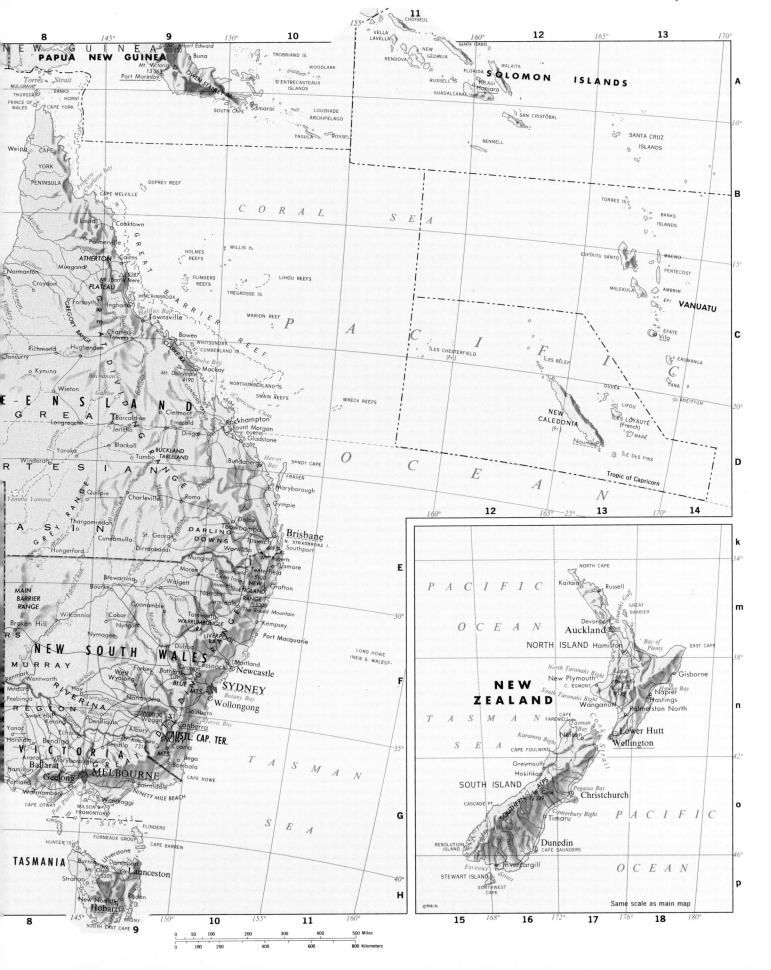

Same scale as main map

North America • *Terrain*

North America has several mountainous areas. The western mountains are made up of two main chains that stretch from Alaska at the northern end of the continent to Panama at the southern end. The Rocky Mountains rise out of the Great Plains. In Colorado, more than fifty of the Rockies are higher than fourteen thousand feet (more than four thousand meters). The Rockies reach into Canada, where they are even more spectacular than they are in the United States.

Many other mountain ranges rise west of the Rockies. Some of them contain volcanoes. Mount St. Helens, an active volcano in Washington, erupted in 1980. It sent steam high into the air and dropped ash many miles away.

The Great Basin lies between the two western mountain chains in the United States. Mountains prevent most of the rain clouds that form over the Pacific from reaching the Great Basin, and the southern end of the basin is a desert. Farther south, a desertlike region covers much of the American Southwest and reaches deep into Mexico.

The two mountain chains extend into Mexico as well. The Sierra Madre Occidental is in the west, and the Sierra Madre Oriental is in the east. Plateau

The Great Plains extend from the southern United States well into Canada. They contain some of the best farmland in the world. Wheat fields in the Canadian province of Saskatchewan are shown below.

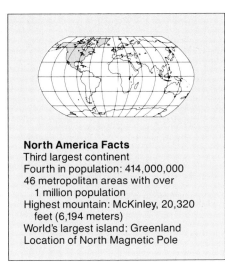

The walls of Arizona's Grand Canyon show different layers of rock. Each layer marks a different period in the earth's history. The layers at the bottom on the canyon are probably more than one billion years old.

country spreads out between them, and it is here that most Mexicans live.

Central America, at the south end of North America, is mainly mountainous. There are many volcanoes here. The small country of Guatemala has more than thirty of them.

The mountains of eastern North America are much lower than the ones to the west. Some of them are older mountains, and they have been worn down by time and weather. One such range is the Appalachians, the biggest mountain range in the eastern United States.

The Great Plains lie at the center of North America. This region is one of the largest plains on earth, and the land is mostly flat or gently rolling as far as the eye can see. The land is also very fertile, and many crops are grown here.

North America has several important rivers and bodies of water. The Mississippi and Missouri rivers form the longest river system on the continent. Lake Superior, one of the Great

Two of North America's most famous volcanoes are in Mexico. According to Mexican folklore, Iztaccihuatl (to the right) was a beautiful woman, and Popocatepetl (to the left) was a warrior who loved her.

Lakes, is the biggest freshwater lake in the world. The Panama Canal, near the southern tip of North America, is a human-made strip of water that is very important. It allows ships to pass between the Atlantic and the Pacific oceans without having to go all the way around the southern tip of South America.

Some of North America lies within an imaginary line called the Arctic Circle, as does some of Europe and Asia. Because of the natural movements of the earth, the sun does not set for one or more days a year north of the Arctic Circle. In this region, the sun stays above the horizon on the longest days of the year, in June. It does not rise at all on the shortest days of the year, in December. The climate north of the Arctic Circle is very harsh.

North America · *Animals*

As the number of people in North America has increased, the number of wild animals has decreased. People have hunted some kinds of animals to extinction, until there are none left. Some animals have become extinct for other reasons. Some animals survive, but their numbers have greatly decreased. In national parks and areas where there are few people, many kinds of animals can still be found. And some animals have adapted to living near people and cities.

The buffalo, or American bison, was once nearly wiped out by hunters. But a few were saved, and today there are thousands of buffalo in national parks.

There are some wolves in the north, and some grizzly bears, too. The bald eagle, the national bird of the United States, is still found in the Northwest. These animals are in danger of becoming extinct in the wild, but they might survive in zoos.

The coyote and the raccoon are two animals that seem to thrive near people. There are many coyotes in the West, and raccoons are found in many places.

Many kinds of rattlesnakes live in North America. The biggest of them is the eastern diamondback, often seven feet (over two meters) long. The coral snake lives in deserts, as does a poisonous lizard called the Gila monster. The armadillo lives nearby.

In the swamps and rivers of the southeastern part of the continent lives the alligator. Sea otters and sea lions live in the ocean off the West Coast. So do some of the biggest of all animals — California gray whales, which may be as much as forty feet (over twelve meters) long.

Here are some animals that are extinct. The numbers tell how long ago they lived. Some animals become extinct naturally, through *evolution*. Such is probably the case with dinosaurs. In recent times, some animals have become extinct because of human interference. The great auk, for example, was wiped out by hunters.

Apatosaurus
135 Million Years Ago

Tyrannosaurus
70 Million Years Ago

Woolly Mammoth
10 Thousand Years Ago

Great Auk
Mid Nineteenth Century

Saber-Toothed Cat
1 Million Years Ago

Passenger Pigeon
Late Nineteenth Century

Grizzly Bear

Walrus

Herring Gull

Canada Goose

Polar Bear

Mountain Goat

Red Fox

Gray Wolf

Rock Ptarmigan

Bald Eagle

Beaver

Porcupine

Mountain Lion

Moose

Robin

King Salmon

Pronghorn

Gray Squirrel

Sea Otter

Elk

Raccoon

White-tailed Deer

Willet

Bison

Cottontail

Gambel's Quail

Diamondback Rattlesnake

Opossum

Turkey

California Sea Lions

Peccary

Alligator

Armadillo

Roseate Spoonbill

Brown Pelican

Squirrel Monkey

Gray Whale

North America · *Life on the Land*

Ice hockey is a popular sport played by both amateurs and professionals in Canada and the United States, as well as in other countries. Hockey is the national sport of Canada.

The United States and Canada, two of the three largest countries in North America, are among the richest nations in the world. Many factors contribute to this abundant wealth, including agriculture.

North America has much fertile farmland and a good climate for growing a variety of crops. Both the United States and Canada grow more than enough food for their people to eat, so they export food to other countries. Farming is done with modern methods and machinery that are very efficient. This means that fewer farmers can grow more crops. For this reason, not many people are farmers in the United States and Canada.

Agriculture is very important in Mexico and in other countries of North America as well. Corn is grown in Mexico. In Central America and the islands called the West Indies, coffee, sugarcane, and bananas are grown. But much of the land in these countries is not good for growing crops, and many of the farmers do not have modern machinery. For these reasons, farming in these countries is not as efficient as it is in countries to the north.

North America is rich in forests and minerals, from which many things can be made. These natural resources have helped the United States and Canada to become world leaders in manufacturing. Many cities in these countries have been huge industrial centers for many years, but this is changing.

There is not as much manufacturing in the other countries of North America, although there is some in Mexico.

According to folklore, the giant Paul Bunyan and his enormous blue ox Babe created much of America's landscape. The legend says they dug the St. Lawrence River in three weeks using a shovel as large as a house.

Greenland

Canneries

Mining

Alaskan
Pipeline

Oil Fields

Salmon Fishing
and Canning

Lumbering

Fur Trapping

Fishing

Totem Pole

Ski Trails

Lumbering

Canadian Wheatlands

Giant Redwoods

Agricultural Area

Mt. Rushmore

Dairyland

Statue of Liberty

Wheat

Potatoes

Agricultural Area

Cars
Manufactured

Soybeans

Washington, D.C.

Truck Farming

Hollywood

Corn

Offshore Oil Drilling

Citrus Groves

Longhorn Cattle

Peanuts

Tobacco

Agricultural Area

Cotton

Citrus Groves

Cape Canaveral

Corn

Oil Fields

Sugarcane

Olmec Sculpture

Ruins of Ancient Pyramids

Sugarcane Made
into Molasses

Agricultural Area

Coffee

Bananas

The famous Ballet
Folklorico of Mexico per-
forms many dances based
on Mexican history and
legend. The dancers below
wear costumes modeled
after those worn by the
Mayas, an Indian people
who lived in Mexico a
thousand years ago.

North America • *Countries and Cities*

Canada's houses of Parliament are in Ottawa, Ontario, the national capital. It is here that Canada's elected leaders meet to govern the country's ten provinces and two territories.

Most of North America is divided among three nations: Canada, the United States, and Mexico. Central America is part of North America. It covers an area less than a third the size of Mexico, and it contains seven countries. Many of the islands of the Caribbean are independent countries, but some of them are governed by bigger countries, such as the United States.

The countries of North America are mainly inhabited by descendants of Europeans who crossed the seas after the 1500s. Native Americans, the people who lived here long before the Europeans arrived, still populate some areas. In some places, they still live in ways that are similar to the ways their ancestors lived.

The boundaries of North American nations have been relatively stable for the last hundred years or so. Many wars were fought in establishing them, however.

The people of most of the countries of North America elect their leaders. The United States and Canada are two such countries. In some countries, such as Panama, military leaders have taken control of the government. Cuba, an island nation in the Caribbean, has a communist government.

The main language of each North American nation is the language spoken in the European country that once dominated the area. For example, Spain once ruled Mexico, and although Mexico is now independent, its people still speak Spanish. Most Canadians speak English as a result of many years of British rule. But some areas of Canada, such as the Province of Quebec, were long dominated by France, so many people speak French. Some Native Americans who live in isolated areas speak the languages of their ancestors.

Cities usually grow up around areas that are accessible to trade routes, and the cities of North America are no exception. Many of them sprung up near bodies of water that were traveled by the many traders who explored the land. For example, Chicago, Illinois, grew up on a crossroads that linked the Great Lakes and the Mississippi River.

Today, some of the biggest and most modern cities in the world are in North America. Mexico City has the second largest population of any city in the world. New York City has the fourth largest.

Roads
Railroads

Mexicans shoot off
fireworks and hold
fiestas to celebrate
Independence Day,
September 16.
Mexico declared its
independence from
Spain in 1810.

Cities,
Towns,
and
Villages

| 0 to 25,000 | ○ | 100,000 to 250,000 | ⊙ | 1,000,000 and over | ◉ |
| 25,000 to 100,000 | • | 250,000 to 1,000,000 | ◎ | Major urbanized area | |

Scale 1:12,600,000; one inch to 200 miles. Conic Projection
Elevations and depressions are given in feet

85°

QUEBEC

Same scale as main map

Gulf of St. Lawrence

LONG RANGE MTS.

CAPE BAULD

GROS MORNE NAT'L PARK

Deer Lake

Botwood   Windsor   Gander   Bonavista

Corner Brook   Grand Falls   TERRA NOVA NAT'L PARK   Trinity

Stephenville

C. ST. GEORGE

St. George's Bay

Red Indian

NEWFOUNDLAND

St. George's   Trinity Bay

CAPE RAY   Channel-Port-aux-Basques   St. John's

Cabot Strait   Fortune Bay   Placentia Bay

CAPE NORTH   Grand Bank   Burin

CAPE BRETON ISLAND   ST. PIERRE AND MIQUELON (Fr.)

ATLANTIC OCEAN

©RMcN

MELVILLE PENINSULA

Gulf of Boothia

Arctic Circle

FRANKLIN

Foxe Basin

BAFFIN ISLAND

Baffin Island Nat'l Park

Pangnirtung

Nettilling

PRINCE CHARLES ISLAND

Amadjuak

Cumberland Sound

CUMBERLAND PEN.

MERCY

Frobisher Bay

HALL PEN.

Lake Harbour   Frobisher Bay

EVERETT MTS.

Igloolik

Wager Bay

SOUTHAMPTON ISLAND

Roes Welcome Sound

Fisher Strait

C. LOW

COATS

MANSEL

NOTTINGHAM ISLAND

SALISBURY

C. DE NOUVELLE-FRANCE

Hudson Strait

RESOLUTION

C. HOPES ADVANCE

AKPATOK

CAPE CHIDLEY

TORNGAT MTS.

Hebron

Ivujivik

Ungava Bay

Nain

PENINSULE D'UNGAVA

Payne

Chimo

Hopedale   Makkovik

Hamilton Inlet

Rigolet   Cartwright

HUDSON BAY

OF KEEWATIN

Povungnituk

OTTAWA ISLANDS

Minto

aux Feuilles

Kaniapiskau

Koksoak

MEALY MTS.

Battle Harbour

NEWFOUNDLAND

Michikamau   Naskaupi

Little Mecatina

St. Anthony

All islands within bays and straits lie within Northwest Territories.

BELCHER ISLANDS

Lac Bienville

LABRADOR

Grande de la Baleine

Caniapiscau

Schefferville

Churchill Falls

Romaine

Natashquan

LONG RANGE MTS.

GROS MORNE NAT'L PARK

Corner Brook   Stephenville   St. George's

C. HENRIETTA MARIA

PTE. LOUIS-XIV

La Grande

Eastmain

Nichicun

MTS. OTISH

Lac Manicouagan

Natashquan

ILE D'ANTICOSTI

Mingan

Gulf of St. Lawrence

Channel-Port-aux-Basques

CAPE BRETON HIGHLANDS NAT'L PARK

James Bay

Ft. George

Rivière de Rupert

Opinaca

Mistassini

Chibougamau

R. aux Outardes

Clarke City   Sept-Îles

Ft. Severn

Severn

Winisk

AKIMISKI

Ft. Albany

QUEBEC

Betsiamites

Cap-Chat   Gaspé

MTS. CHIC-CHOCS   Chandler

Matane   PEN. DE GASPÉ   New Carlisle

Mont-Joli   Caraquet

Rimouski   ILES DE LA MADELEINE

Moosonee

Nottaway

Dolbeau   Kenogami

St. Félicien   Alma   Chicoutimi

Roberval   Jonquière   Chambord   Saguenay   La Malbaie

Trout Lake   St. Joseph

Coral Rapids   Fraserdale

Missinaibi

Mattagami

Réservoir Gouin

St. Maurice   Baie-St. Paul

Rivière-du-Loup

Edmundston   Bathurst

Campbellton   NEW BRUNSWICK

Newcastle   Richibucto

P.E.I.

Summerside   PRINCE EDWARD ISLAND NAT'L PARK

Charlottetown

Red Lake

ONTARIO

Armstrong Sta.   Nakina

Hearst

La Sarre   Amos   Senneterre

Rouyn   Malartic   Val-d'Or

Moncton   Amherst

Fredericton   Sackville   Springhill   Stellarton   NOVA SCOTIA

FUNDY NAT'L PARK   New Glasgow   Sydney Mines

Oromocto   Truro   Sydney

Kenora   Sioux Lookout   Geraldton   Longlac   Oba   Kapuskasing   Cochrane

Iroquois Falls   Timmins   Kirkland Lake   Ville-Marie   Shawinigan

Grand-Mère

Trois-Rivières   Victoriaville

Joliette   Sorel   Drummondville

Woodstock   Saint John   Windsor

St. Andrews   Kentville   Yarmouth

St. Stephen   St. George   Digby

Bay of Fundy   Bridgewater

Dryden   Nipigon   Longlac

Cobalt   Témiscaming

St. Hyacinthe   Granby   SHERBROOKE   Lac-Frontière

Lunenburg   Liverpool

Shelburne

CAPE SABLE

Nipigon   Chapleau

MONTRÉAL   St-Jean   Sorel

Lennoxville   Megantic   MAINE

Kenora   Dryden   Marathon

PUKASKWA NAT'L PARK

MICHIPICOTEN I.

Sudbury   Sturgeon Falls   North Bay   Mattawa   Pembroke   Ottawa   Hull   Laval   Valleyfield

Montmagny

Thunder Bay

Sault Ste. Marie   Thessalon   Blind River   Espanola   MANITOULIN I.   Parry Sound   Huntsville   Renfrew   Smiths Falls   Brockville   Ogdensburg   Alexandria Bay   Concord

Sault Ste. Marie

Lake Superior

Georgian Bay

Lake Huron

Wiarton   Midland   Orillia   Peterborough   Kingston   Cobourg   Lindsay   NEW YORK

VERMONT   NEW HAMPSHIRE

MASS.   Hartford   Providence

R.I.

Lake Champlain

Montpelier

Duluth   Superior   Marquette   Escanaba

MICHIGAN

Owen Sound   Barrie   Simcoe   Oshawa   Whitby   Lake Ontario   Albany

CGNN.   Portland

BOSTON   CAPE COD

MINNESOTA   WISCONSIN   Green Bay

Lake Michigan

TORONTO   Hamilton   Rochester

Kitchener   St. Catharines   Niagara Falls   BUFFALO   NEW YORK

London

St. Paul   Madison   Milwaukee   Saginaw   Flint   Lansing   Grand Rapids

Sarnia   Chatham   Port Huron   St. Thomas

NEW YORK

PENNSYLVANIA   Scranton   Newark   N.J.

MINNEAPOLIS   Mississippi   DETROIT   Windsor   Lake Erie   Leamington   OHIO

ILL.   CHICAGO   Toledo

ATLANTIC OCEAN

Gulf of St. Lawrence

Channel

A-520200-26-4-9-8-17
COPYRIGHT BY
RAND McNALLY & COMPANY
MADE IN U.S.A.

40,000 SQ MI AREA

0   100   200
Miles

0   25 50 75 100   200   300   400   500 Miles

0   100   200   400   600   800 Kilometers

Scale 1:12,600,000; one inch to 200 miles. Polyconic Projection
Elevations and depressions are given in feet

12

40,000 SQ MI
AREA
0   100   200
Miles

**Cities
and
Towns**

0 to 50,000   500,000 to 1,000,000

50,000 to 500,000   1,000,000 and over

Scale 1:17,200,000; one inch to 270 miles. Polyconic Projection
Elevations and depressions are given in feet

ATLANTIC OCEAN

Aguadilla · Arecibo · San Juan
PTA. HIGUERO · Utuado · Bayamón · CABEZAS DE SAN JUAN · ST. THOMAS · TORTOLA (Br.)
PUERTO RICO · Caguas · Fajardo · CULEBRA · Charlotte Amalie · ST. JOHN (U.S.A.)
Mayagüez (U.S.A.) · Coamo · Cayey · Humacao · Vieques · VIEQUES
CABO ROJO · Ponce · Salinas · Guayama
CARIBBEAN SEA · Christiansted · SAINT CROIX (U.S.A.)

Scale 1:4,300,000
0 10 20 30 40 Miles
0 10 20 30 40 50 60 Kilometers
©RMcN.

LITTLE HANS LOLLICK
OUTER BRASS · HANS LOLLICK
INNER BRASS · PICARA PT · GRASS CAY
STORMY PT. · STORMY PT. · THATCH CAY
ST. THOMAS
Crown Mt. (U.S.A.) 1558 · Charlotte Amalie (St. Thomas) · Nadir
WATER · St. Thomas Harbor
FLAMINGO PT.
Scale 1:540,000
©RMcN.

ATLANTIC OCEAN

NORTH AMERICAN BASIN

KY · W.VIRGINIA · Roanoke · Richmond
VIRGINIA · Norfolk
Knoxville · Raleigh · Chesapeake Bay
NORTH CAROLINA · CAPE HATTERAS
Mt. Mitchell 6684 · Charlotte
ATLANTA · SOUTH · Wilmington
GEORGIA · Columbia · CAROLINA
Augusta · Charleston · CAPE FEAR
Savannah
Tallahassee · Jacksonville
St. Augustine
FLORIDA · Ocala · CAPE CANAVERAL
Tampa · Tampa Bay
W. Palm Beach
MIAMI · GRAND BAHAMA · GREAT ABACO
CAPE SABLE · BAHAMAS · ELEUTHERA
Key West · Nassau · CAT
FLORIDA KEYS · ANDROS · LONG
Straits of Florida
HAVANA · Guanabacoa · Matanzas · SAN SALVADOR (WATLING)
Marianao · Cárdenas · ACKLINS
Pinar del Río · Santa Clara · CAICOS · TURKS
CUBA · Sancti Spíritus · Nuevitas · GT. INAGUA
Cienfuegos · Ciego de Ávila · Camagüey
Trinidad · Holguín · PUERTO RICO TRENCH
ISLA DE LA JUVENTUD · Manzanillo · Guantánamo · PUNTA MAISÍ · Cap-Haïtien · Puerto Plata · 28 374
GRAND CAYMAN (Br.) · SIERRA MAESTRA · Santiago de Cuba · Santiago de los Caballeros · C. SAMANA · Mayagüez · San Juan
C. CRUZ · Gonaïves · Sánchez · C. ENGAÑO · Ponce · Charlotte Amalie · VIRGIN IS. · ST. THOMAS · ANGUILLA (Br.)
Montego Bay · Mt. Denham 3236 · Port Antonio · ÎLE DE LA GONAVE · Pico Duarte 3.417 · PUERTO RICO (U.S.A.) · BARBUDA (Ant.)
Spanish Town · Port-au-Prince · Santo Domingo · SAINT CROIX (U.S.A.) · ST. CHRISTOPHER-NEVIS · ANTIGUA
JAMAICA · Kingston · HISPANIOLA · MONTSERRAT (Br.) · V. Soufrière 4869 · Pointe à Pitre · GUADELOUPE (Fr.) · Basse Terre
ANTILLES · DOMINICA
MARTINIQUE (Fr.) · Fort-de-France
SAINT LUCIA
WINDWARD IS. · SAINT VINCENT · BARBADOS
Kingstown · Bridgetown
GRENADA
CARIBBEAN SEA · LESSER
PUNTA DE GALLINAS · ARUBA (Neth.) · PUNTA DE PARAGUANA · CURAÇAO BONAIRE (Neth.) (Neth.) · TOBAGO
PENÍNSULA DE GUAJIRA · PEN. DE PARAGUANA · Willemstad · ISLA LA TORTUGA · ISLA DE MARGARITA · TRINIDAD AND TOBAGO
Santa Marta · Golfo de Venezuela · Coro · Puerto Cabello · La Guaira · Carúpano · Port of Spain
Barranquilla · Ciénaga · Maracaibo · San Felipe · CARACAS · Cumaná · TRINIDAD
Cartagena · Soledad · Cabimas · Maracay · Puerto La Cruz · Maturín
AMERICA · Lago de Maracaibo · Valencia · Barquisimeto
Bluefields · Lago de Nicaragua
COSTA RICA · San José · Limón · Colón · Portobelo · Golfo del Darién · Lorica · Sincelejo · Mompós · Trujillo · Guanare · Calabozo · El Tigre · Morawhanna
Cartago · Golfo de los Mosquitos · PANAMÁ · Golfo de Darién · Magangué · Valera · San Fernando de Apure · Orinoco
RICA · David · Antón · PEN. DE AZUERO · Panamá · Montería · Mérida · Puerto de Nutrias · Ciudad Guayana
COIBA · Santiago · Golfo de Panamá · Ocaña · CORDILLERA DE MÉRIDA · Cerro Bolívar · Ciudad Bolívar
Golfo Dulce · Barrancabermeja · Cúcuta · San Cristóbal · VENEZUELA · Cerro Icutu 7800
Pamplona · Arauca · Salto Angel
Bucaramanga · Meta
Medellín · Tunja · San Fernando de Atabapo · GUYANA
Sonsón · Río Orinoco
Manizales · COLOMBIA · Ventuari
Pereira · Tolima 7.110 · BOGOTÁ · Guaviare · SERRA PACARAIMA
ISLA DE MALPELO (Colombia) · Armenia · Ibagué · Girardot · Villavicencio · San Fernanda de Atabapo
Buenaventura · Cali · Palmira · Guaviare · Río Orinoco · BRAZIL

40 000 SQ MI AREA
0 100 200 Miles

0 50 100 200 300 400 500 Miles
0 100 200 400 600 800 Kilometers

Cities and Towns
0 to 50,000 · 500,000 to 1,000,000
50,000 to 500,000 · 1,000,000 and over

South America · *Terrain*

High in the Andes lies Lake Titicaca, South America's largest lake. This lake has been a center of Indian civilization for hundreds of years. These men are fishing as their ancestors did.

The Andes Mountains run down the entire western side of South America. Stretching more than four thousand miles (about 6,500 kilometers), the Andes chain is the longest in the world. This range also has some of the world's tallest peaks. Only the Himalayas in Asia are higher. There are several smaller mountain ranges in South America, especially in the eastern part of Brazil.

Where Argentina, Bolivia, and Chile meet, the Andes split into two ranges. They are separated by a plateau about four hundred miles (about 650 kilometers) wide. This is called the *altiplano*, or high plateau. It is nearly two and a half miles (about four kilometers) above sea level and is almost perfectly flat.

In northern Chile, between the Andes and the Pacific, is the Atacama Desert. This desert is near the ocean, yet it is one of the driest spots on earth. In some parts of the Atacama, no rainfall has ever been recorded.

The Amazon River begins in the Andes of Peru and flows almost four thousand miles (more than six thousand kilometers) to the Atlantic Ocean. The Amazon contains more water than any other river on earth. Over four million cubic feet (more than 113,000 cubic meters) pour out of the Amazon and into the Atlantic each second. The fresh water from the river can be detected in the salt water of the ocean for about a hundred miles (160 kilometers) off the coast of South America.

The Amazon flows out of a huge plain called the Amazon River basin, an area almost as big as the United States. The equator runs through this area, so it is very warm, and it receives a lot of rainfall. These factors combine to make this jungle region the biggest tropical rain forest on earth.

Another plain stretches across Paraguay and most of Argentina. It is made up of two different areas — the Gran Chaco and the Pampa. The Gran Chaco is a dry region with few trees. The Pampa receives more rain; it is a nearly treeless grassland that is ideal for cattle and sheep grazing. Patagonia lies near the southern tip of South America. It is drier than the Pampa, but it, too, is a sheep-grazing area.

At the very tip of South America is a group of islands called Tierra del Fuego, which means "land of fire." Long ago, when Spanish explorers sailed past these islands, they saw fires that the inhabitants had lighted. The explorers named the islands after these fires.

Most of South America has a tropical climate. In the Andes, however, the climate changes as you go higher. At the very tops of the mountains, only the toughest of plants can grow.

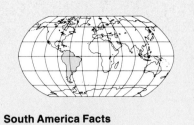

South America Facts
Fourth largest continent
Fifth in population: 282,200,000
28 metropolitan areas with over
  1 million population
Highest mountain: Aconcagua, 22,831
  feet (6,959 meters)
World's highest waterfall: Angel Falls,
  3,212 feet (979 meters)
Equator passes through

The Atacama Desert,
in northern Chile,
is bordered on the
west by low
mountains and on
the east by the
high Andes. There
is little life on
the desert because
it is one of the
driest spots on
earth.

The Amazon River
contains more water
than the Nile,
Yangtze, and
Mississippi rivers
combined. And only
the Nile is longer
than the Amazon.
The bends in the
river are called
meanders.

South America · *Animals*

Nearly a fourth of all species of animals known to people live in South America. But as in other parts of the world, people are hunting these animals and using the lands the animals live on, so many creatures are in danger of becoming extinct.

The Amazon jungles provide homes for many animals. The jaguar, a big spotted cat, lives here. So does the tapir, an animal that looks like a big pig, with a longer nose. In the many trees of the jungle are parrots, macaws, toucans, and different kinds of monkeys. Sloths hang upside down from the trees. They are *nocturnal*, meaning that they come out only at night. Giant snakes such as the anaconda and the boa constrictor also live in these jungles. In the waters are flesh-eating piranhas and electric eels, which stun their prey with electric shocks.

On the plains of South America live giant anteaters, which may be more than six feet (about two meters) long. Maned wolves live here, too. They look like foxes walking on stilts.

In the Andes live llamas, vicuñas, and alpacas. Some of these animals have been tamed by people who use them like sheep or cattle. The spectacled bear lives on the mountain slopes. It gets its name from the circles of yellowish fur, like eyeglass frames, around its eyes. The great South American condor also lives in the Andes. Its wings spread up to ten feet (about three meters).

The Galápagos Islands lie about six hundred miles (almost one thousand kilometers) off the coast of Ecuador. Here live species of animals, such as the giant tortoise, that are not found anywhere else. Some of the animals have been wiped out, but the islands are now a national park and wildlife refuge.

Sloth
Tapir
Manatee
Scarlet Ibis
Coatimundi
Ocelot
Toucan
Piranha
Green Turtle
Spectacled Bear
Caiman
Anaconda
Spider Monkey
Red Brocket Deer
Vampire Bat
Llama
Howling Monkey
Capybara
Jaguar
Macaw
Chinchilla
Great Anteater
Vicuña
Brazilian Lapwing
Condor
Guanaco
Maned Wolf
Alpaca
Blue Marlin
Torrent Duck
Pampas Deer
Rhea
Elephant Seal
Magellan Goose
Magellan Penguin
Cavy
Black-necked Swan
Sperm Whale

South America · *Life on the Land*

Close to half of all South Americans make their living by farming. Most farms are quite small and can produce only enough food for the families that own them. Most of these people use old-fashioned ways of farming, with no machinery.

There are huge, modern farms and ranches, however, and they are owned by a small number of wealthy people. Some of these farms are larger than many of the states of the United States. These farms grow huge quantities of coffee, wheat, sugar, bananas, and other food. Most of the food is *exported*, or sold to other parts of the world.

Herds of sheep and beef cattle are raised on giant ranches. Argentina is one of the largest producers of beef in the world, and it exports more beef than any other country. It is also a large producer of wool.

There are many large, modern cities in South America, and industry is increasing. But South America is still far behind Europe and North America in manufacturing.

Life in the big cities of South America is much like life in the cities of North America. There are tall, modern buildings, airports, and busy streets. But many of the Indians outside of the cities of Peru, Bolivia, and Ecuador still live the way their ancestors lived, in tiny villages where there are only dirt roads and no electricity. And in the Amazon jungle, many small groups of people still live by hunting and farming, as they have for thousands of years.

Over four hundred years ago, the empire of the Incas thrived in the Andes. Legend has it that the first Incas, Manco Capac and his sister, were created by the sun god on the Isle of the Sun in Lake Titicaca.

Soccer, or *fútbol* in Spanish, is one of the world's most widely played sports. It is the national sport of several South American countries.

Weaving is an age-old art in the Andes, one passed down from generation to generation. Indians spin thick alpaca wool into yarn to make warm blankets, hats, and other clothing.

Oil Exported

Oil Fields

Mining

Coffee Bean Farming

Emerald Mining

Fishing

Shipping

Agricultural Area

Cotton

The Amazon

Rubber

Mahogany Logging

Brazil Nuts Harvested

Spanish-style Architecture

Indians of Peru

Agricultural Area

Machu Picchu (Inca Ruins)

Fishing in Lake Titicaca

Soccer

Anchovy Fishing

Brasília

Mining

Mining

Trees Tapped for Tannin

Light Industry

Rio de Janeiro

Coffee Grown

Copper

Agricultural Area

Cattle Raising

Beef for Export

Fishing

Wheatlands

Bonito Fishing

Lumbering and Sawmills

Sheep Herding

South America · *Countries and Cities*

Just like North America, South America was explored and conquered by Europeans after about 1500. People from Spain, Portugal, and other European countries took over the land, some of which had been inhabited by Indians for many years. Many wars were fought over the years, but the borders of many of today's South American countries have existed for over one hundred years.

Sometimes, when a country is undergoing troubles, military leaders will take control of the country. This has happened in many South American nations at different times. Today, some South American countries remain under military rule. Paraguay and Chile are two such countries. The people of other countries, such as Argentina and Brazil, have recently elected their leaders.

South America's largest and most populated country is Brazil. Only the Soviet Union,

High in the Andes near Cuzco, Peru, lie the ruins of Machu Picchu, which was probably the last Inca hideaway. It remained unknown to the Spanish conquerors; white people did not find it until 1911.

China, Canada, and the United States are bigger in area than Brazil. More people live in Brazil than in all other South American countries combined. Brazil is also the leading industrial country of South America.

Argentina is the second largest South American country in both area and population. It has many more people than any of its smaller neighbors.

The more northern countries of Peru, Ecuador, and Bolivia have much in common. They all once belonged to the empire of the Incas, a highly civilized people that lived in South America before Europeans arrived. Cuzco, in modern-day Peru, was the capital of the empire. An ancient fortress still stands in the city. Its walls are made of boulders so big that scientists cannot understand how the Incas were able to build with them.

Like North Americans, most South Americans speak the language of the European country that once ruled the area in which they live. For example, Brazil was once a colony of Portugal, and today most Brazilians speak Portuguese. Many other South American countries were once dominated by Spain, and Spanish is widely spoken on the continent. Suriname was a colony of the Netherlands, however, and the people there speak Dutch. The people of Guyana speak English, as the nation was once under British rule.

There are many Indians in South America who still speak the languages of their ancestors.

South America has many important cities. The biggest of them is Sao Paulo, Brazil. It is the third largest city in the world. Buenos Aires, Argentina, and Rio de Janeiro, Brazil, are also in the world top ten in population. All three cities are very modern and have a lot of industry. If you look at these three cities on the map, you see they all have something in common: they are all near the Atlantic coast. They all grew up around or very close to natural *ports*, or places where ships could safely land. Many cities around the world have been established near such ports.

Brasilia, the capital of Brazil, was built in the 1950s and 1960s. The city is well planned and has much modern architecture.

Mining is Chile's most important industry. Not only does it bring the country money from exports, but it also employs many people.

NICARAGUA

CARIBBEAN SEA

PACIFIC OCEAN

ARCHIPIELAGO
DE COLON
(GALÁPAGOS ISLANDS)
(Ecuador)

VENEZUEL

CARACAS

COLOMBIA

MEDELLIN

BOGOTA

Cali

Popayán

ECUADOR

Quito

Guayaquil

Cuenca

Iquitos

PERU

LIMA

Callao

Chimbote

Trujillo

Chiclayo

AMAZO

SELVAS

ACRE

RONDÔ
(TER.)

BOLIV

La Paz

Sucre

Potosí

CHILE

Antofagasta

ARGENTINA
SALTA

Tropic of Capricorn

A-549100-26   9-8-16*
COPYRIGHT BY
RAND McNALLY & COMPANY
MADE IN U.S.A.

Scale 1:16,850,000 ; one inch to 265 miles. Sinusoidal Projection
Elevations and depressions are given in feet

Longitude West 65° of Greenwich

Cities
and
Towns

0 to 50,000

50,000 to 500,000

500,000 to 1,000,000

1,000,000 and over

MEDELLIN

ANTIOQUIA

CORDILLERA OCCIDENTAL

CORDILLERA CENTRAL

CALDAS

RISARALDA

CHOCÓ

Quibdó

Manizales

Pereira

Armenia

QUINDIO

Ibagué

TOLIMA

VALLE DEL CAUCA

Cali

Palmira

Buga

CUNDINAMARCA

BOGOTÁ

Girardot

CORDILLERA ORIENTAL

META

HUILA

Neiva

Scale 1:4,200,000

0   10   20   30   40 Miles

0 10 20 30 40 50 60 Kilometers

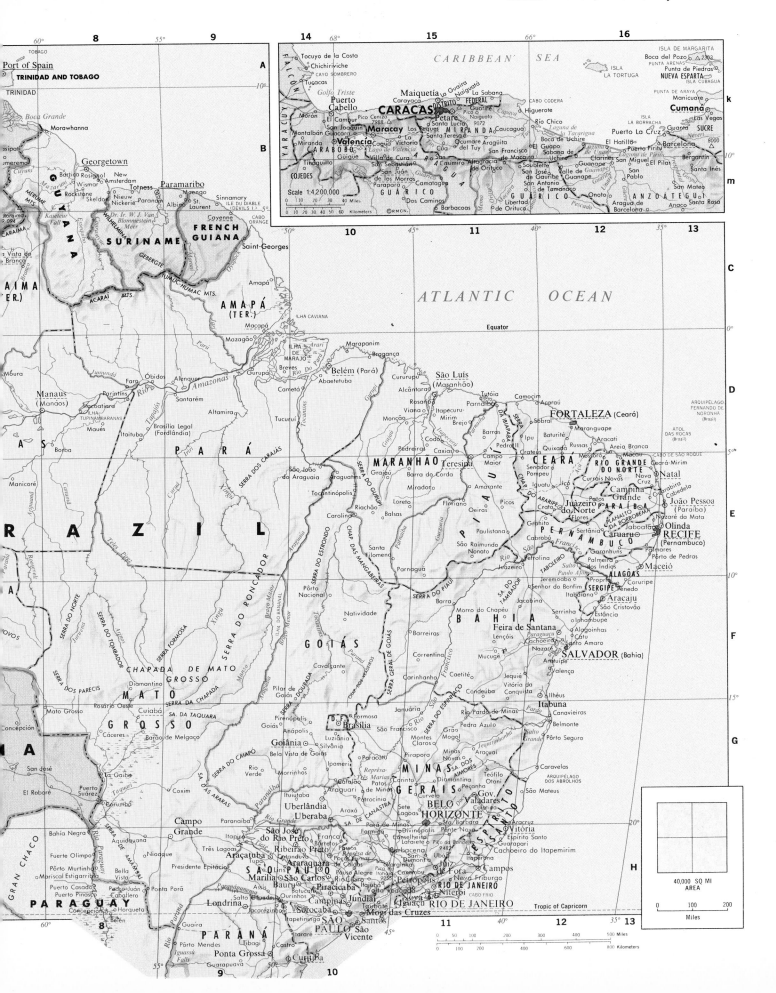

Inset map (Venezuela — Caracas region)

CARIBBEAN SEA

FALCON
Tocuyo de la Costa
Chichiriviche
CAYO SOMBRERO
Tucacas
Golfo Triste
Puerto Cabello
Morón
Montalbán Guacara
Miranda
San Joaquín
Valencia
Guigue
Tinaquillo
COJEDES
El Cambur Pico Ceniza 7988
La
San Sebastián
Villa de Cura
San Juan de los Morros
Parapara
Dos Caminos
CARABOBO
Maracay
Cagua La Victoria
Maiquetía La Guaira Naiguatá La Sabana
Carayaca
DISTRITO FEDERAL
CARACAS
Petare
Santa Lucía 9072
Guatire
Pico d'la Silla
Ocumare del Tuy
Santa Teresa
Cúa
San
A
G
U
A
ISLA DE MARGARITA
Boca del Pozo 2303
PUNTA ARENAS
Punta de Piedras
NUEVA ESPARTA
ISLA CUBAGUA
PUNTA DE ARAYA
Manicuare
Cumaná
Las Vegas
SUCRE
ISLA LA BORRACHA
Puerto La Cruz Guanta
Puerto Pirítu
El Hatillo
Clarines San Miguel El Pilar
Barcelona 8000
Bergantín
Santa Inés
San Mateo
Santa Rosa
CABO CODERA
Higuerote
Río Chico
Laguna de la Tacarigua
Boca de Uchire
El Guapo
Capaya
MIRANDA
Los Teques
Caucagua
Araguita
Altagracia de Orituco
El Sombrero
Sabana de Uchire
Soublette
San José de Gauribe
San Antonio
Valle de Guanape
GUARICO
Onoto
Aragua de Barcelona
Anaco
ANZOATEGUI
GUARICO
Camatagua
Libertad de Orituco
Barbacoas
San Pablo
Laguna de Unare
Pescado

Scale 1:4,200,000
0 10 20 30 40 Miles
0 10 20 30 40 50 60 Kilometers
©RMCN.

Main map

TOBAGO
Port of Spain
TRINIDAD AND TOBAGO
TRINIDAD
Boca Grande

Morawhanna
Georgetown
MERUME MTS.
Bartica Rosignol New Amsterdam
Wismar Nieuw Nickerie
Rockstone Skeldon
Totness Paramaribo
Moengo St. Laurent
Nieuw Albina
Paranam

GUYANA
Mazaruni
Cuyuni
Roraima 9.094
CARAIMA (TER.)
Vista do Branco

WILHELMINA
Dr. Ir. W. J. Van Blommestein Meer
SURINAME
GEBERGTE
FRENCH GUIANA
Cayenne
ILE DU DIABLE (DEVIL'S I.)
Sinnamary
CABO ORANGE
Saint-Georges
ACARAÍ MTS.
TUMUC-HUMAC MTS.

ATLANTIC OCEAN

AMAPÁ (TER.)
Amapá
Macapá
Mazagão
ILHA CAVIANA
Equator

Manaus (Manáos)
Itacoatiara
ILHA TUPINAMBARANAS
Maués
Borba
Parintins
Óbidos Alenquer
Faro
Santarém
Brasília Legal (Fordlândia)
Itaituba

B R A Z I L

P A R Á
Breves
ILHA DE MARAJÓ
Gurupá
Belém (Pará)
Abaetetuba
Cametá
Tucuruí
Altamira

Marapanim
Bragança
Cururupu
São Luís (Maranhão)
Alcântara
Viana
Rosário
Itapecuru-Mirim
Monção
Codó
Caxias
Pedreiras
Carolina
Balsas
Loreto
Riachão
Santa Filomena

MARANHÃO
Teresina
Barra do Corda
Grajaú
Mirador
Floriano
Oeiras
Picos

Tutóia
Parnaíba
Camocim
Sobral
Ipu
Baturité
Quixadá
Crateús
Campo Maior
Barras
Pedro II
Iguatu
Granito
Paulistana
São Raimundo Nonato
Parnaguá

FORTALEZA (Ceará)
Maranguape
Aracati
Russas Areia Branca
Macau CABO DE SÃO ROQUE
Ceará-Mirim
CEARÁ
RIO GRANDE DO NORTE
Nova Cruz Natal
Currais Novos
Patos
Campina Grande
Juàzeiro do Norte
Crato
PARAÍBA
João Pessoa (Paraíba)
Nazaré da Mata
Caruaru
PERNAMBUCO
Olinda
RECIFE (Pernambuco)
Garanhuns Palmares
Cabrobó Sertânia
Petrolina
Salto Paulo Afonso dos Índios
TABOLEIRO
Maceió
ALAGOAS
SERGIPE
Aracaju
Jeremoabo
Propriá
Senhor do Bonfim
Corupibe Penedo
Itabaiana
São Cristóvão
Jacobina
Serrinha
Santa Luzia
Inhambupe
Alagoinhas
Catu
Santo Amaro
São Francisco
Salto Grande

ATOL DAS ROCAS (Brazil)
ARQUIPÉLAGO FERNANDO DE NORONHA (Brazil)

PIAUÍ
CHAP. DO ARARIPE
PLANALTO DA BORBOREMA
CHAPADA DO APODI

BAHIA
Feira de Santana
Cachoeira
Nazaré
Mucugê
Lençóis
Barreiras
Correntina
Carinhanha
Caetité
Jequié Vitória da Conquista
Morro do Chapéu
Itaberaba
Serra do Tombador

SALVADOR (Bahia)
Amargosa
Valença
Ilhéus
Itabuna
Canavieiras
Belmonte
Pôrto Seguro
Caravelas
ARQUIPÉLAGO DOS ABROLHOS

GOIÁS
Natividade
Cavalcante
Pôrto Nacional
Pilar de Goiás
Barra

MATO GROSSO
CHAPADA DE MATO GROSSO
Diamantino
SERRA DA CHAPADA
Mato Grosso
Rosário Oeste
Cuiabá
Cáceres
Barão de Melgaço
SERRA DOS PARECIS
Concepción
San José
La Gaiba
El Robore
Puerto Suárez
GRAN CHACO

PARAGUAY
Bahía Negra
Fuerte Olimpo
Pôrto Murtinho
Mariscal Estigarribia
Puerto Casado
Bella Vista
Concepción
Horqueta
Belén

MINAS GERAIS
Formosa
D.F. Brasília
Luziânia
Silvânia
Anápolis
Goiânia
Bela Vista de Goiás
Ipameri
Paracatu
Rio Verde
Morrinhos
Catalão
Araguari
Uberlândia
Uberaba
Araxá
SA. DE CANASTRA
Sete Lagoas
BELO HORIZONTE
Pará de Minas
Divinópolis
Formiga
Montes Claros
Grão Mogol
Minas Novas
Diamantina
Curvelo
Pirapora
São Francisco
Januária
Rio Pardo de Minas
Pedra Azul
SERRA DO ESPINHAÇO
Grão Mogol
Teófilo Otoni
Peçanha
Gov. Valadares
Colatina
Sta. Bárbara
Ponte Nova
SERRA DOS AIMORÉS
Caratinga
São Mateus
Aracruz
ESPÍRITO SANTO
Vitória
Espírito Santo
Guarapari
Cachoeiro do Itapemirim
9482
Pico da Bandeira

Campo Grande
Aquidauana
Nioaque
Coxim
Corumbá
Três Lagoas
Presidente Epitácio
Paranaíba

SÃO PAULO
São José do Rio Prêto
Araçatuba
Marília
Bauru
Araraquara
São Carlos
Piracicaba
Campinas
Jundiaí
Sorocaba
Mogi das Cruzes
Itapetininga
Franca
Barretos
Ribeirão Prêto
Botucatu
Ourinhos
Assis
SÃO PAULO
Santos
São Vicente
Ituiutaba
Frutal
Passos
Poços de Caldas
Pouso Alegre
São João del Rei
Barbacena
Varginha
Lavras
Itajubá 9255
Cambuquira
Juiz de Fora
Barra Mansa
Volta Redonda
Campos
Nova Friburgo
Niterói
RIO DE JANEIRO
CABO FRIO
Petrópolis
RIO DE JANEIRO
Ubá
Itaperuna
Petrópolis

PARANÁ
Londrina
Tibagi
Castro
Ponta Grossa
Guarapuava
Iguaçu Falls
Pôrto Mendes
Guaíra
Curitiba

Rivers and features
Amazonas Rio
Tapajós
Xingu
Araguaia
Tocantins
Parnaíba
São Francisco
Paraná
Paraguay
Rio Grande
Negro
Teles Pires
Juruena
SERRA DOS CARAJÁS
SERRA DO GURUPI
SERRA GERAL DE GOIÁS
SERRA DO ESTRONDO
CHAP. DAS MANGABEIRAS
SERRA DO RONCADOR
SERRA FORMOSA
SERRA DO CAIAPÓ
SERRA DO PIAUÍ
Tropic of Capricorn

Scale bars
0 50 100 200 300 400 500 Miles
0 100 200 400 600 800 Kilometers

40,000 SQ MI AREA
0 100 200 Miles

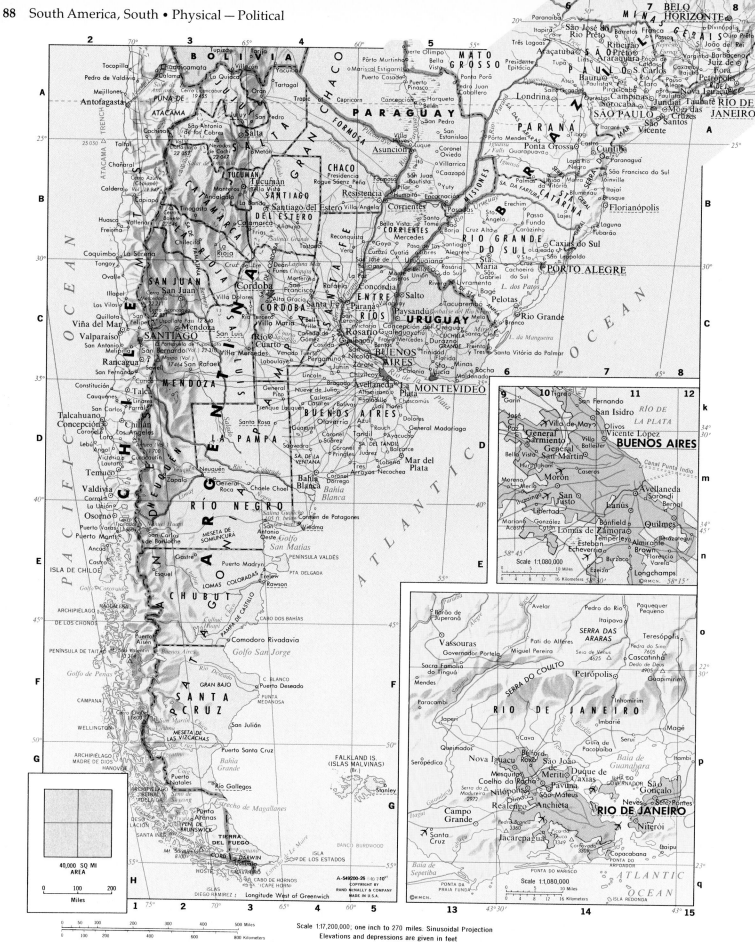

Scale 1:17,200,000; one inch to 270 miles. Sinusoidal Projection
Elevations and depressions are given in feet

40,000 SQ MI AREA

0   100   200
Miles

BUENOS AIRES
Scale 1:1,080,000

RIO DE JANEIRO
Scale 1:1,080,000

Antarctica

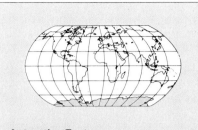

Antarctica Facts
Fifth largest continent
No permanent population
Highest mountain: Vinson Massif,
   16,067 feet (4,897 meters)
Location of South Pole
Location of South Magnetic Pole
World's lowest recorded temperature:
   Vostok, −129°F (−89.5°C)

Antarctica, the coldest continent on earth, is at the South Pole. It is so cold here that a person without the right kind of clothing would freeze to death in a matter of minutes. In mid-winter, which is June in the Southern Hemisphere, temperatures may drop below −100 degrees Fahrenheit (−73 degrees Celsius). Like some places north of the Arctic Circle, Antarctica is without sunlight for part of the year. This happens because of the natural tilt of the earth.

Most of Antarctica is covered with snow so thick, it forms a mile-high plateau at the South Pole. In many places, the snow has been packed by its own weight and frozen to become a massive ice pack. This ice is so heavy, it has pressed parts of the land way below sea level. If the ice cap melted, all that could be seen of Antarctica above the water would be a mountain chain that crosses the continent.

Many warm-blooded animals live in the waters that surround Antarctica. Among these are seals, birds, and great blue whales. Antarctica is the home of many penguins. Though penguins are birds, they cannot fly. Their wings are used as paddles to help them swim.

In 1911, explorers discovered the South Pole. Over the years, many other explorers and scientists have gone to Antarctica, but no people make their permanent home there. Today, many nations claim parts of Antarctica. According to a treaty among the nations, claims can be settled in 1989.

Because of its formidable climate, Antarctica was the last continent to be explored. Early visitors used dog sleds such as this one, but today motorized toboggans are more common.

World Facts and Comparisons

General Information

Mean distance from the earth to the sun, 93,020,000 miles.

Mean distance from the earth to the moon, 238,857 miles.

Equatorial diameter of the earth, 7,926.38 miles.

Polar diameter of the earth, 7,899.80 miles.

Mean diameter of the earth, 7,917.52 miles.

Equatorial circumference of the earth, 24,901.46 miles.

Polar circumference of the earth, 24,855.34 miles.

Total area of the earth, 197,000,000 square miles.

Total land area of the earth (incl. inland water and Antarctica), 57,900,000 square miles.

Highest elevation on the earth's surface, Mt. Everest, Asia, 29,028 feet.

Lowest elevation on the earth's land surface, shores of the Dead Sea, Asia, -1,312 feet below sea level.

Greatest known depth of the ocean, southwest of Guam, Pacific Ocean, 35,810 feet.

Area of Africa, 11,700,000 square miles.

Area of Antarctica, 5,400,000 square miles.

Area of Asia, 17,400,000 square miles.

Area of Europe, 3,800,000 square miles.

Area of North America, 9,400,000 square miles.

Area of Oceania (incl. Australia) 3,300,000 square miles.

Area of South America, 6,900,000 square miles.

Population of the earth (est.1/1/89), 5,192,000,000.

Principal Islands and Their Areas

Island	Area (Sq.Mi.)
Baffin I., Can.	195,928
Borneo (Kalimantan), Asia	287,300
Celebes (Sulawesi), Indon.	73,057
Corsica, France	3,352
Crete, Greece	3,189
Cuba, N.A.	42,800
Cyprus, Asia	3,572
Great Britain, U.K.	88,795
Greenland, N.A.	840,000
Hainan Dao, China	13,100
Hawaii, U.S.	4,034
Hispaniola, N.A.	29,300
Hokkaidō, Japan	32,245
Honshū, Japan	89,176
Iceland, Europe	39,800
Ireland, Europe	32,600
Jamaica, N.A.	4,200
Java (Jawa), Indon.	51,038
Luzon, Philippines	40,420
Madagascar, Africa	227,000
Mindanao, Philippines	36,537
Newfoundland, Can.	42,031
New Guinea, Oceania	309,000
Puerto Rico, N.A.	3,500
Sakhalin, Sov. Un.	29,500
Sardinia, Italy	9,301
Sicily, Italy	9,926
Southampton I., Can.	15,913
Spitsbergen, Norway	15,260
Sri Lanka, Asia	24,900
Taiwan, Asia	13,900
Tasmania, Austl.	26,200
Tierra del Fuego, S.A.	18,600
Vancouver I., Can.	12,079
Victoria I., Can.	83,897

Principal Lakes, Oceans, Seas, and Their Areas

Lake/Country	Area (Sq.Mi.)
Arabian Sea	1,492,000
Arctic Ocean	5,400,000
Atlantic Ocean	31,800,000
Baltic Sea, Eur.	163,000
Bering Sea, Asia–N.A.	876,000
Black Sea, Eur.-Asia	178,000
Caribbean Sea, N.A.–S.A.	1,063,000
Caspian Sea, Iran–Sov. Un.	143,240
Chad, L., Cameroon–Chad–Nig.	6,300
Erie, L., Can.-U.S.	9,910
Great Salt Lake, U.S.	1,680
Hudson Bay, Can.	475,000
Huron, L., Can.-U.S.	23,000
Indian Ocean	28,900,000
Mediterranean Sea, Eur.–Afr.–Asia	967,000
Mexico, Gulf of, N.A.	596,000
Michigan, L., U.S.	22,300
North Sea, Eur.	222,000
Ontario, L., Can.-U.S.	7,540
Pacific Ocean	63,800,000
Red Sea, Afr.–Asia	169,000
Superior, L., Can.-U.S.	31,700
Tanganyika, L., Afr.	12,350
Titicaca, Lago, Bol.–Peru	3,200
Victoria, L., Ken.–Tan.–Ug.	26,820
Yellow Sea, China–Korea	480,000

Principal Mountains and Their Heights

Mountain/Country	Elev. (Ft.)
Aconcagua, Cerro, Arg.	22,831
Annapurna, Nepal	26,503
Apo, Phil.	9,692
Ararat, Turkey	16,804
Blanc, Mont (Monte Bianco), France–Italy	15,771
Bolívar (La Columna), Ven.	16,411
Cameroon Mtn., Cam.	13,451
Chimborazo, Ecuador	20,561
Citlaltépetl, Mex.	18,701
Cook, Mt., New Zealand	12,349
Cristóbal Colón, Pico, Colombia	19,029
Dhaulāgiri, Nepal	26,810
Elbert, Mt., Co., U.S.	14,431
El'brus, Gora, Sov. Un.	18,510
Elgon, Mt., Kenya–Uganda	14,178
Etna, Mt., Italy	10,902
Everest, Mt., China–Nepal	29,028
Fairweather, Mt., Canada	15,300
Fuji-san, Japan	12,388
Gannett Pk., Wy., U.S.	13,785
Gongga Shan, China	24,902
Grand Teton Mtn., Wy., U.S.	13,766
Grossglockner, Austria	12,461
Hood, Mt., Or., U.S.	11,239
Illimani, Nevado, Bol.	21,151
Iztaccíhuatl, Mex.	17,343
Jaya, Puncak, Indon.	16,503
Jungfrau, Switz.	13,642
K2 (Godwin Austen), China–Pak.	28,250
Kānchenjunga, India–Nepal	28,208
Kātrīnā, Jabal, Egypt	8,652
Kilimanjaro, Tanzania	19,340
Kirinyaga (Mt. Kenya), Kenya	17,058
Kommunizma, Pik, Sov. Un.	24,590
Kosciusko, Mt., Austl.	7,316
Koussi, Emi, Chad	11,204
Lassen Pk., Ca., U.S.	10,457
Logan, Mt., Canada	19,520
Longs Pk., Co., U.S.	14,255
Margherita, Zaire–Uganda	16,763
Matterhorn, Italy–Switz.	14,685
Mauna Kea, Hi., U.S.	13,796
Mauna Loa, Hi., U.S.	13,680
McKinley, Mt., Ak., U.S.	20,320
Misti, Volcán, Peru	19,098
Mulhacén, Spain	11,424
Nānga Parbat, Pak.	26,660
Nevis, Ben, U.K.	4,406
Ólimbos, Greece	9,570
Pikes Pk., Co., U.S.	14,110
Popocatépetl, Volcán, Mex.	17,887
Rainier, Mt., Wa., U.S.	14,410
Sajama, Nevado, Bol.	21,463
Shasta, Mt., Ca., U.S.	14,162
Toubkal, Jebel, Morocco	13,665
Triglav, Yugo.	9,393
Vesuvio (Vesuvius), Italy	3,842
Vinson Massif, Antarc.	16,864
Washington, Mt., N.H., U.S.	6,288
Whitney, Mt., Ca., U.S.	14,494
Wilhelm, Mt., Pap. N. Gui.	14,793

Principal Rivers and Their Lengths

River/Continent	Length (Mi.)
Amazonas–Ucayali, S.A.	4,000
Amu Darya, Asia	1,578
Amur, Asia	2,744
Arkansas, N.A.	1,459
Brahmaputra, Asia	1,770
Colorado, N.A. (U.S.–Mex.)	1,450
Columbia, N.A.	1,200
Congo (Zaïre), Africa	2,900
Danube, Europe	1,776
Euphrates, Asia	1,510
Ganges, Asia	1,560
Huang (Yellow), Asia	3,395
Indus, Asia	1,800
Irrawaddy, Asia	1,300
Lena, Asia	2,700
Limpopo, Africa	1,100
Loire, Europe	625
Mekong, Asia	2,600
Mississippi, N.A.	2,348
Missouri, N.A.	2,315
Murray, Australia	1,566
Negro, S.A.	1,300
Niger, Africa	2,600
Nile, Africa	4,145
Ohio, N.A.	981
Orange, Africa	1,300
Orinoco, S.A.	1,600
Paraguay, S.A.	1,610
Paraná, S.A.	2,800
Peace, N.A.	1,195
Pechora, Europe	1,124
Plata–Paraná, S.A.	3,030
Red, N.A.	1,270
Rhône, Europe	500
Rhine, Europe	820
Rio Grande, N.A.	1,885
São Francisco, S.A.	1,988
Salween (Nu), Asia	1,750
Saskatchewan–Bow, N.A.	1,205
Snake, N.A.	1,038
St. Lawrence, N.A.	800
Sungari (Songhua), Asia	1,140
Syr Dar'ya, Asia	1,370
Tarim, Asia	1,328
Tennessee, N.A.	652
Tigris, Asia	1,180
Tocantins, S.A.	1,640
Ucayali, S.A.	1,220
Ural, Asia	1,509
Uruguay, S.A.	1,025
Volga, Europe	2,194
Xingú, S.A.	1,230
Yangtze (Chang), Asia	3,900
Yellowstone, N.A.	671
Yenisey, Asia	2,543
Yukon, N.A.	1,770
Zambezi, Africa	1,700

Index of Major Places on the Physical-Political Maps

For instructions on using the map keys, see page 9.

Map Names and Abbreviations

This table lists the names and the abbreviations used for features on the physical-political maps. Each entry includes the feature name, the language from which it comes, and, in the case of foreign names, its English translation. Abbreviations are shown for those names that are abbreviated on the maps.

Ákra (Greek): cape, *Akr.*
Cabo (Spanish, Portuguese): cape, *C.*
Cap (French): cape, *C.*
Cape (English): *C.*
Cerro (Spanish): mountain, hill
Cordillera (Spanish): mountain chain, *Cord.*
Erg (Arabic): strait
Estrecho (Spanish): strait
Fort (English): *Ft.*
Golfo (Spanish, Italian): gulf, bay, *G.*
Gora (Russian): mountain, *G.*
Gulf (English): *G.*
Hai (Chinese): sea
Île (French): island
Ilha (Portuguese): island
Isla (Spanish): island, *I.*
Jabal (Arabic): mountain
Khrebet (Russian): mountain range
Lake (English): *L.*
Lago (Spanish, Portuguese): lake, *L.*
More (Russian): sea
Mountain(s) (English): *Mt. (Mts.)*
Mys (Russian): cape, *M.*
National (English): *Nat'l*
Occidental (Spanish): western

Oriental (Spanish): eastern
Óros (Greek): mountain
Ozero (Russian): lake, *Oz.*
Peninsula (English): *Pen.*
Peski (Russian): desert
People's Democratic Republic (English): *P.D.R.*
Plato (Russian): plateau
Point (English): *Pt.*
Pointe (French): point, *Pte.*
Poluostrov (Russian): peninsula, *P-Ov.*
Proliv (Russian): strait
Punta (Spanish): point
Reservoir (English): *Res.*
Río (Spanish): river, *R.*
River (English): *R.*
Salto (Spanish, Portuguese): waterfall
Serra (Portuguese): mountain chain, *Sa.*
Shan (Chinese): mountain, hill
Sierra (Spanish): mountain range, *Sa.*
Sound (English): *Sd.*
Soviet Socialist Republic (English): *S.S.R.*
Vodokhranilishche (Russian): reservoir, *Vdkhr.*
Volcano (English): *Vol.*

OCEAN
HORIZON
ICEBERG
CRATER
DORMANT
VOLCANO
ATOLL
ARM
FJORD
POINT
BAY
SUMMIT
GLACIER
SNO
TIMBER
TIMBER
STRAIT
ARCHIPELAGO
CHANNEL
DELTA
TOWN
PLAIN
REEF
SOUND
BLUFF
WAVES
CAPE
CLIFF
SPIT
SEA
SANDBAR
GULF
KNOB
KNOLL
GROVE
BREAKERS
BEACH
SHOAL
INLET
PENINSULA
ISTHMUS
LAGOON
PASTURE
HEADLAND
RIVER
BAYC
PRECIPICE
LEVEE
RAILROAD
SHORE LINE
CITY
AND
BREAKWATER
HARBOR
WHARF
DOCK
SEAPORT
BRIDGE
ISLAND
RIVER
MOUTH
CULTIVATED LAND
ESTUARY
PIER
DIKE
AIRPORT
ROAD
HIGHWAY
FIELD
MEADOW